SEO

FOR BEGINNERS

The Ultimate Beginner's Guide to Get 500 Visitors a Day and Rank No. 1 on the Internet

BRIAN WOOD

TABLE OF CONTENTS

TABLE OF CONTENTS

iv

CHAPTER ONE

Introduction to SEO (Search Engine Optimization)

What is SEO?

SEO (Search Engine Optimization) has to do with the science or process, and in some cases, the art of ensuring websites are well visible on search engines in results generated and get the maximum relevant traffic to the website. This is why "optimization" is used. This process involves so many more processes than anyone could have imagined, from the site's structure, the manner and way in which other websites connect to it, and the words mentioned in major areas of the site.

This knowledge is well-known and has been proven that the earlier and higher up a particular website is ranked or appears on search pages, the higher the traffic to be delivered by users of these search engines to that website.

Another factor influencing traffic is how frequent your content appears on result pages or the number of times that the website pops up on the results page of search engines. The main goal of SEO is to get the best of appearance as well as direct more traffic to a website through a search engine.

Search engines make use of Internet bots referred to as 'spiders' or 'crawlers' to help to index websites on the web and then ensure their indexes are kept updated. This process is referred to as crawling or to clarify better; crawling has to do with cataloging and reading websites on the Internet.

Note that SEO has to do with improving the natural or organic results generated by the search engines for one's website. What we mean by organic here is that these results are not optimized via paying search engines to do the job like those of ad-based optimization to achieve sponsored or paid results, which has to do with different tactics or strategies, and some payments made. Altogether, this is another process of search engine methodology.

Before we continue to explain the ways in which SEO achieves the objectives mentioned above for a particular website, let us consider a very important question: Why is SEO necessary for a website to begin with?

Why is it Important?

Although generating traffic is necessary and possible, as well as building interest and getting recognition for your website through advertising, social media, as well as other traffic forms to help attract visitors to your site, search engines form the major backbone of visibility and publicity of a website. This has to do with two main reasons:

First, search engines can be referred to as the virtual highways through which most of the traffic of the Internet flows and locates its destinations. Forbes revealed that at the close of 2013, 40% of all the traffic on the Internet was made through Google. So if your website doesn't do well when it comes to search engines, it is missing out on a whole lot of traffic on the Internet.

Second, a very important quality of any search engine is able to generate as well as direct some traffic to a website. In other words, what we mean is that visitors who have much interest in what a particular website offers. These visitors, who search engines, deliver websites to, form a large part of a website's success and growth on the web since in most cases as they form the basis of publicity,

revenue, as well as exposure to a level that no marketing type can match or compensate for. Therefore, investing in search engine optimization is very important to the prosperity of any venture on the Internet due to the stakes associated with it.

Common Techniques of SEO

SEO (Search Engine Optimization) doesn't completely involve complex methods dealing with comprehending the anatomy and algorithms of the Internet. A huge part of it is composed of techniques that are very easy to use and understand, which could be used by anyone, average webmasters or Internet-savants.

Before we proceed, there's a need to comprehend that SEO has to do with search engine marketing (SEM). This comprises SEO as well as paid advertising, SEO being organic reach or natural and paid advertising makes use of paid reach to ensure a website's visibility is increased. In some cases, these two intertwine and overlap, because they seem to both have the same goals.

When we talk of SEO, there's a need to differentiate between off-page and on-page SEO. These two cannot be separated from search engine optimization; however, the difference has to do with where these SEO techniques are applied. On-page optimization has to do with optimizing elements on a specific page, which means the optimization of websites based on SEO guidelines. Off-page SEO, on the other hand, has to do with using different techniques in a bid to optimize a website utilizing external elements that include link-building as well as nurturing your website's reputation.

The classification of SEO techniques is done in many ways; however, one classification is of procedural or legal nature. And this is white-hat SEO versus black-hat SEO with grey-hat SEO standing just in between the two.

Blackhat SEO has to do with those techniques disapproved by search engines and not tolerated in some cases, which could cause some websites to be penalized, meaning they lose rankings, or they are removed completely from results generated by the search engines. All of them have something in common; they revolve around tricking or deceiving both the search engine and its algorithms into delivering better results and higher ranking for that website. They are not focused on generating better content and creating committed content visitors or user base. They are focused on getting to the top of the search results using different tricks. Black-hat SEO, for instance, involves using the same color for the background, and the text itself hidden in it.

Another inevitable and obvious characteristic is black-hat SEO in most cases, which is a short-term enterprise and only delivers short term gains, whereas results from white-hat SEO delivers long-lasting results and are more focused on creating reliable and better content as well as building and serving a wider user base. White-hat SEO is also viewed as optimization performed in line with guidelines put in place by the search engines.

Below is a list of the common SEO techniques employed:

- Ensuring the website is stocked with rich keywords as well as key phrases to accommodate as many queries as possible. It deals with adding relevant keywords to a website's metatags

- Creating a unique and dense title tag for each page. This assists search engines in comprehending a page's content by providing a quick reference for them.

- Creating media content like newsletters, e-zines, or press clippings, to maintain inbound links

- Maintaining the saturation of search engines optimally and regularly comparing with competitor sites. Search engine saturation has to do with denoting the number of pages a particular website already indexed by the search engines. This measures how efficient the efforts of optimization have been and marks the accessibility and visibility of the site effectively.

- Making use of online resources like Google Analytics and Google Trends to comprehend online patterns and behaviors in the whatever is trending

- Different search phrases and making sure they are employed in the content's first one hundred words

- Including a backlink for any web directory

- Using 301 directs or canonical metatags to achieve the normalization of URL in cases of multiple URL web pages.

- Crosslinking between pages on a particular website

- Provision of a large number of links to the website's main pages.

- Making use of other websites that link to the original

- Using a mixture of key phrases and keywords to go in line with the business/brand being promoted.

Creating Contents as an SEO Technique

Aside from these techniques, the creation of content is the basis of white-hat SEO. There's no website that can prosper, even minimally without content with novelty, uniqueness, relevance, and value. All these elements in total must be combined in any content that can be scanned easily. White-hat SEOs majorly rely on what we refer to as linkbait; this is a technique where the creation of content is done to be shared on a large scale expecting to earn backlinks.

The SEO of today is based on users. This is why content plays a significant role in SEO. The creation of outstanding content will help in the attraction of users, which will inform search engines that your website offers lots of value, and so, therefore, raises your website's ranking.

The final category here is the grey-hat SEO, which comes in the form of a boundary between the white-hat and black-hat SEO. These SEO techniques carry the risk of being penalized and disapproved by search engines but technically are not against the parameters and guidelines that were set by the search engines. One good example of grey-hat SEO is creating microsites that are owned by one webmaster and then linking them back to the main website, which is where you want the optimization to take place.

SEO Used as a Marketing Strategy

One significant use of SEO is using it as a form of a marketing strategy for entrepreneurs and businesses. Having better rankings and visibility on search engines could make a lot of difference in a business achieving success when we talk of having an edge and getting ahead in the competitive markets of today on the Internet.

One simple way of comprehending this is to see the Internet as a complex network of roads, while the search engines are the major highways where drivers discover places and navigate their route to places having something to offer them. Search results revealed on Yahoo or Google are just like highway signposts – they reveal to you what is present somewhere and helps users to access places they did not even know about.

Entrepreneurs could create a website that is relevant, very attractive, and user-friendly with content having even demand. However, if there's no way users or consumers can access it or even know about it, it is just like a proverbial tree that makes no sound while falling in

6

a forest. Therefore, when we talk about e-commerce, the currency behind the success of a business on the web is traffic.

The more your page is discovered by people, the more the likelihood of being frequent visitors, which will then convert them into consumers of what your website is offering, be it a product or service, or whether it's just information you're selling.

SEO is a way of enhancing your relationship with the different search engines out there to make you as visible as possible. Investing in SEO comes with a lot of benefits, and organizations/businesses achieve significant results in revenue and popularity after including SEO in their marketing strategy.

However, over-reliance on SEO to generate revenue and traffic comes with a downside, due to the fact that the search engines constantly alter their algorithms and evolve their systems of ranking and crawling. This is why when SEO is used as a tool for marketing. It then becomes an endeavor that requires constant analysis and vigilance. However, there are more benefits compared to the pitfalls, which is why trends and statistics in e-commerce are beginning to bear testimony as to how effective SEO is as a marketing tool.

For instance, in 2012, the online market of India surpassed the $150 million mark, where half of this was accounted for by search engines. This tells us how important the use of search engines is in attracting consumers to your website. Therefore, a website that fails to be optimized to perform well in search engines is already losing about 50% of the possible traffic it could generate.

Importantly, SEO is a form of Internet marketing, and this is why it overlaps other Internet marketing forms like social media marketing and paid advertising. For instance, in paid advertising, SEO helps in creating a landing page that will end up affecting the results of paid advertising. Social media marketing, on the other hand, seems to send signals (termed social signals), which may affect search engines in the process of determining to rank.

Although this may be the case, we are sure that when a search engine is used for a particular query, lots of results obtained from social networking websites will be seen, most especially if these are popular accounts having lots of followers and activities. Therefore, most times, we see results from Twitter, Facebook, and Wikipedia, as well as other social networks, rank high in pages of search results, which backs the idea that social media marketing plays a vital role in improving a website's visibility on the Internet, achieving the same goal as that of SEO.

CHAPTER TWO

❖·+·———————·❖·+·❖·+·❖·—————————·+·❖

Understanding Search Engines

How Search Engines Work

Though search engines are majorly just Internet navigators, it would be very unrealistic to imagine the existence of the Internet without them. As a result of the absolute depth and size of the World Wide Web, this handy information becomes unusable and meaningless without the presence of search engines. Basically, three tasks are performed by search engines:

- The use phrases of specific words in searching the World Wide Web

- The results found as well as their locations are indexed

- User access is offered to this index as well as the ability to search for it making use of combinations of desired phrases or words

Search engines today perform about ten million queries each day, and they constantly evolve and reinvent their services to go in line with the needs of advertisers, users, and websites.

It begins with something referred to as spiders (also known as crawlers) and how great, knowing fully well that the Internet is referred to as the World Wide Web. Spiders are referred to as robots or inter-bots made up of coding or software. Internet spiders, just like real spiders do something referred to as web crawling or simply crawling to make a long list of whatever is found on the Internet.

Crawling is referred to as an act of copying, indexing, and browsing done by the spiders. They begin with a well-known website (the web's busy part) or a heavily used server and then crawl outwards to whatever link is found on the server or website behaving just like real spiders when they spread.

Though Google was the first to bring up the spider idea, using this has become well known across the community of search engines, and the desire is always to create newer, more creative, and faster spiders.

Everything we read is indexed by spiders, making use of something referred to as metatags, which are explanations of phrases or keywords under which the owner of the website would like the indexing of his or her website to be done. They assist these spiders in understanding what the page deals with and where it can be located in an index.

Webmasters may utilize descriptions or words in metatags that are not accurate or reference well-known keywords and topics which may be difficult for their website to handle. To fight against this, spiders are brought in to correlate these metatags with website content and then come up with an understanding of where the page should be on an index.

Another large organ in search engine anatomy is the algorithm used. Algorithms have to do with computer coding or software designed to take those words inputted into the search bar and then deliver results that are most relevant from the indexes made by these spiders. They turn search engines into an answering machine. They depend on clues or signals from websites indexed to come up with search result rankings.

These signals vary in the freshness of the content on the website, the number of times it was visited recently, and that particular region where the user is making this query belongs. Google is known to make use of about 2000 different signals in assisting its algorithms in the creation of search listings each time the search button on the computer is tapped.

How Users Interact with Search Engines

The secret to designing as well as improving any service or product is considering the human aspect of the interaction of real people with it. If there's a need to come up with a marketing strategy that focuses on search engine marketing and SEO, it starts with understanding the way and manner in which users interact with these search engines. Users can only be given what they desire if you have an idea of what it is, and what they are getting already and how best you want to improve on it.

Search Engine Figures and Facts

Let us begin by having some understanding of some figures and figures about people and search engines, so we have an idea of where we stand. As of 2011, about 59% of Internet users utilize search engines on a daily basis, which is just about an inch of the most used Internet application as of today, known as an email that accounts for about 61% of users on a daily basis.

This tells us how the dominance and reliance on the activities of search over the activities of other Internet are on the rise. As revealed by StatsCounter, the largest market share is held by Google, sending about 91% of traffic, followed by Yahoo! at 3.78% and then Bing at 3.72%.

UserCentric also carried out a study demonstrating that users tend to concentrate more on organic results compared to sponsored or paid results, and there's a higher chance to click organic results compared to sponsored results. Interestingly, advertisements, as well as sponsored results, tend to get equal and, in some scenarios, get more attention when they pop up first in organic results.

Another discovery from this study was that users tend to pay little or no attention to what is found at the bottom of the page compared to what appears on top. The same way, descriptions, and keywords that are written in bold tend to receive more attention as well as click-through rates compared to just simple text, most especially if it is located below the page.

Search Engine Marketing (SEM)

SEM, which is also called search engine marketing is an Internet marketing that deals with the promotion of websites and making them more visible by either the website structure themselves and optimizing the content and how they perform in search engines, or by making use of advertising and buying sponsored results. The final goal is getting higher rankings in searches, be more visible, and gain some new traffic while keeping old users. This has turned into a big market in itself. In North America, about $19 billion was spent by advertisers on the Internet in the year 2012.

The greatest vendors of online marketing with search engines are Bing Ads, Baidu, and Google AdWords. Agencies majorly for advertising have started specializing in SEM due to the fact that this form of Internet marketing is growing very fast and even surpassed some traditional types of advertising. Though, the majority of campaigns are performed through agencies and vendors, SEM tools and self-serve solutions can be found online as well. SEM has now covered a wide range of marketing activities that are related to search engines, which include managing sponsored listings, submitting websites to directories, and creating marketing strategies to ensure the success of organizations, individuals, and businesses operating through the web.

Marketing through search engines has to do with:

- Natural or organic results: The improvements of these results are made possible through search engine optimization; this is exactly what we are talking about in this book.

- Paid results: Here, advertising programs are utilized in the promotion of websites in result pages of search engines.

Therefore, marketing using search engines has to do with different tasks that will promote the website, whether they are paid or organic results. Below are some significant tasks involved in the whole process.

Keyword Analysis

This has to do with analyzing keywords in order to find relevant keywords, which are responsible for the greatest traffic for a service or product. For instance, making use of studio flats or keyword studio apartments will be made based on the activity involved in keyword analysis as well as how to trend on the Internet.

The Popularity of the Site

This has to do with the measure of the presence or weight carried by a website on different search engines. This is measured by search engine saturation, which indicates how much indexing is performed on a given website by spiders and the number of backlinks present on a website.

HTML Tools and Web Analytics

This refers to the website's backend or the invisible part of the website to users. It includes web analytic tools that help in measuring, analyzing, and logging file analyzers to other complex ones such as page tagging that makes use of an image or a JavaScript to follow users' actions on a page. Spider-simulators and HTML validators are tools that function in optimizing a site's hidden areas for issues as well as those regarding usability. They ensure that all pages conform to the code standards of the W3C.

Sponsored Results

This deals with purchasing places or purchasing advertisements on pages of search engines to achieve higher views in the section of sponsored results and involves the PPC (Pay-Per-Click) solutions that are provided by the search engines.

Why is search engine marketing important?

With the Internet, there's a unique quality in e-commerce over other traditional business forms, and this is how it is based on new, creative, and entertaining content as well as reduced startup costs. You only need a great idea as well as little cash to start making some money on the Internet.

To be successful in any Internet business, it entails attracting a large number of visitors to a website, and this can only be possible when you deliver great content and make it very accessible to a large number of users. All websites and businesses on the Internet are usually struggling for the best visibility.

Here are the reasons why SEM is so important these days.

First, everyone makes use of search engines, as discussed earlier, to the extent that it is already becoming the Internet's most popular activity. This is why it is the major battleground for the resources and attention of Internet users. With SEM, your website is taken out of your hands and then set in front of a large Internet community – the users of search engines.

Users of the Internet have clouded their minds with the idea that businesses or websites that don't show up on search engines are not legitimate. No website can have this legitimacy factor unless it engages in SEM and is visible on search engines.

With SEM, you are free to do whatever you like with your page because your site can be self-supporting through the income obtained from traffic. There's no need to sell anything. You can have a website or blog about any topic of your choice or offer any service desired without getting worried about giving support to the website.

SEO and SEM are advertising forms that are available to all and can be used in promoting your website without getting any assistance from anyone, or you can request the services of a professional or an agency to help you in this regard. The optimization and marketing will just continue itself if it is properly done and regular enough, so far, your contents are still on the web and in a particular location.

Lastly, if you're an Internet organization, public individual, business, or interest group, you can be very sure that any of your competitors out there are involved in both SEO and SEM.

CHAPTER THREE

Design and Development of the Website

Before we start talking about website development and design that works fine for search engines, it is important to consider one thing. We don't see any particular website the same way, as search engines do. To us, a content might seem important and amazing, while it is not interpretable or is meaningless for a search engine. This is linked to what we discussed earlier, indexing and spiders. When we talk of being comprehended by spiders or being indexed, some contents are simply better than others.

Indexable Content

Though web-crawling has now become a complex task, it is yet to go that far to see the web through the eyes of humans and will need some help along the way. Therefore, all development and design must be done considering what World Wide Web seems to look like to search engines. The world has to be seen through a robot's eyes or that of a software, so as to develop websites that are friendly to search engines and have an inbuilt long-term optimization, rather than having to rely on a few keywords here and few tweaks there, which can only help your SEO for a very short period say weeks, months maximum.

It is very important to consider that despite how much spiders have advanced, they just do great in picking content that is mostly XHTML and HTML, so your elements' website that is most important to you must be in HTML code. Flash images, files, or Java applets are not well-read or understood by spiders. So, your website could have a great design, with amazing contents found outside the

HTML code, and it won't be picked by search engines simply because what these spiders are searching for is in the HTML text.

However, few things could be done to make videos, images, or Java applets present on your website become a content that is indexable or get involved in the business of indexing. First, if any of these images are found in PNG, GIF, or JPG format, which you want the spiders to discover and index, then they need to be included in the HTML by including alt attributes to them as well as give the search engine a brief explanation or description of what the image is all about.

Second, the contents found in the Java plug-ins or Flash may still count by including some text on the page, which explains what the whole content is all about.

Thirdly, if your website contains an audio or video content that you feel is important and should be indexed, those contents you feel users should find, you have to present a transcript of the phrases on search engines to go in line with the video or audio content.

Remember, if this cannot be read by your spider, then the search engines will not feed it to the users. To make your content visible to search engines, there is a need to index them. Different tools are available to achieve this like Google's cache or SEO-browswr.com to help view a website via the search engines' view and then see how a spider sees the site. With this, users will understand what could be going wrong and what others are doing to get it right when it has to do with being noticed by the search engines.

One way to view the content via the search engine 'eyes' is having access to your website's cached version.

Title Tags

Title tags, which are also referred to as the title element, are technically one very important thing to present before a spider and algorithm of any search engine. Ideally, it should be brief and should give a good description of what the website deals with and content hope to be found by the users.

Title tags are not just great for search engines, but they provide users with lots of benefits. Three major dimensions in which value is generated from title tags exist, and this includes browsing, relevancy, and the results produced by the search engines.

Typically, search engines don't just deal with the introductory 50 to 60 words present in your title tag, so you have to be very careful of how long your title tag is. Take note that title tags are not an introduction to a website, rather they are the summary responsible for bringing in potential visitors as well as assisting search engines in comprehending a website's relevance in relation to the keywords present in queries made on search engines by different users. You might have to extend the limit to attain higher rankings if you make use of multiple keywords, and the best advice is to go longer.

Another trick to help in rankings is to try as much as possible to bring those important keywords closer to the beginning or start of your title tag. This will help to increase the possibility of users clicking through your website when your age pops up on search results.

SEO industry leaders conducted a survey which revealed that 94% of the participants revealed that the best place to fix in keywords is the title tag so as to help deliver higher rankings. This is why it is very important to work with title tags that are descriptive, creative, keyword-rich, and relevant. They are referred to like your site's soul expressed in very few sentences (about one or two), and possibly, this could be the only thing the majority of users will have of your site unless they decide to visit it.

One thing that can be done to increase the chances of better rankings via the title tag is by using what we call leverage branding. This entails making use of a brand name right at the end of the title tag. With this, you'll achieve better click-through rates with those people who know that particular brand already or they relate to it.

Meta Tags

Meta tags help in giving instructions, descriptions, as well as providing information to the search engines and different other clients concerning a webpage. They are included as part of the website's XHTML or HTML code, as well as the head section. Different types of Meta tags exist, and they are all important depending on the type of Meta tag.

All the Meta tags cannot be understood by all search engines. For instance, the Meta tags will be ignored by Google if it does not understand or recognize it. There's either very little or no use fixing keywords in the metadata with the hopes of getting higher rankings. Below are some important Meta tags and what can be achieved using them.

Spider Tags

This can be used to influence Internet spiders' activity on each page

Noindex/index: Tells the search engine if a certain page should be indexed or not. Normally, there's no need telling the search engine to index all the pages you are working with; you'll probably be making use of the index option.

Nofollow/follow: This will permit a search engine to either follow a particular page or not whenever it crawls.

Noarchive: With this, you're telling the search engine not to save the cache copy of a given page.

Noodp/noydir will inform an engine not to choose a description for the page using either Yahoo! Or the Open Directory Project.

Meta Description (the description Meta tag)

This gives a summary of your page, thereby informing search engines what a particular page is all about, and in some cases, it comes up as a snippet underneath the title of a website on the results page of search engines. Keywords included in the metadata, in most cases, has nothing to do with rankings. The best thing is to stay within the 160-character limit when writing a Meta description as it is recommended by the W3C.

Link Structure

Link structure is very important for spiders of search engines so as to crawl through the website easily and locate all the links contained in your website. This means your website must possess a link structure that is friendly for search engines and is carved out with spiders in mind. If crawlable or direct links that point to specific pages in your site are absent, they might not exist as well, no matter how great the content on your websites are the spiders won't even get close to it. It is surprising the way websites having great content makes the big mistake of possessing a link structure with navigation that makes it quite difficult or impossible for some parts of the website to pop up on search engine results.

So many reasons account for the inability of certain parts of the pages or a website to show on search engines. Below are some of the most common reasons.

First, if the content on your site can only be accessed after certain forms are submitted, then spiders will most likely have no access to the contents of these pages, and therefore will not show in search engines. If this form requires users to login using a username and password, then input a few details, put in answers to some questions, these spiders will be excluded, since normally they make no efforts to submit forms. This content turns out as invisible.

Secondly, spiders don't really crawl pages effectively, especially those having Java links and pay even less attention to those links embedded within the page. It's best to utilize HTML instead or use it with Java anywhere applicable. This also goes for links in Flash and other plug-ins.

Third, the Meta tag of the robots, as well as the robots.txt file, is used in influencing the spiders' activity and restrict it. Ensure that the pages you want the spiders to disregard have laid down a directive for these spiders to follow. Unintentional tagging has led to the demise of so many great pages.

The fourth reason behind a spiders' broken link structure is search forms. There are millions of pages of hidden content located behind a website's search form, and this will be invisible to search engines because whenever spiders are crawling, they don't perform searches. So users will have to link these contents to a page that is already indexed; this will help locate this content during web crawling.

Fifth, avoid creating links in iFrames or frames unless you have a deep technical understanding of how search engines follow and index links on a page. Though technically speaking, they can be crawled; they pose serious structural issues as well as those linked to the organization.

Finally, links may be ignored or are less accessible if they are present on pages having hundreds of them, due to the fact that spiders only crawl and index a part to protect rankings and fight against spam. The best thing is to ensure that those links that are very important are found on organized and clean pages and then placed in a structure that is clear enough for spiders to locate and index.

Nofollow Links

A lot has to be said concerning the debate about nofollow links and trying to understand what they really mean could be confusing

Let us begin by considering what follows links refer to. Each time someone visits your page or website through a link, this page or website gets a bit of what is called linkjuice by SEO professionals. Also, you can imagine points being given to the link. The number of inbound links your website or page gets will determine the number of SEO points attained as well.

Search engines find this very desirable because they discover that if many people are linking to your website, then it has to be something of value, and thus the website or page will be given much preference in search results.

Linkjuice flows just like real juice. It transfers from one website to the other. For instance, if the National Geographic website links to your page, this means you'll get lots of points or linkjuice than if a small blog mentions your website using a hyperlink; this is because National Geographic is a wide Internet destination, and of course, will get lots of PageRank and juice.

This is exactly where nofollow links are relevant and why the SEO world has seen it as very significant as well as yielding better rankings. Although search engines, in most cases, tend to dismiss the attributes applied to links, generally, they respond to the rel="nofollow" tag. The Nofollow links prevent search engines from following some links, however some act otherwise. It also sends a clear message to indicate pages that shouldn't be seen and read as normal.

Nofollow links began as a method to avoid spam generated automatically, blog entries, as well as some link injection; however, over time, it has now transformed into a tool that permits search engines to disregard some pages as well as transfer any link value. When a nofollow tag is placed on any given link, search engines read and treat them differently compared to other pages that are followed links.

Having a good or even a little quantity of nofollow links to your page or website is not a bad thing, as the majority of those highly ranked or popular websites generally, will have large amounts of inbound follow links compared to their lower-ranked and less popular colleagues. This has to do with having a large portfolio of links that will make up your page or website.

Google has confirmed that in most cases, it doesn't follow nofollow links, and they prevent them from anchoring text or transferring PageRank. In the web graph, no significance is given to the nofollow links; they are usually seen as carrying no weight and therefore believed to be just HTML text. However, many webmasters have this belief that the search engines consider nofollow links, especially those from websites with high authority, as a sign of trust.

Use of Keywords

Keywords seem to be the most significant element in any search activity. They are fundamental parts of indexing, query, and retrieving the information that would not be possible without them. Imagine that 25 different words are used just to describe car tires. Trying to generate traffic to your website through search engines would be very stressful and tiring because you'll miss out on a lot of users dealing with car tires, just because you have failed to use the right keywords used by these people to rank for car tires.

As search engines crawl, they index the web, making use of keywords to form indices. Depending on the specific word, each keyword has millions of pages compared to only thousands that are relevant to the keyword.

If you consider Bing or Google as a huge palace and websites seen as people, then keywords are the different rooms having door tags, and the job is now left in the hands of the spiders to place the relevant people in those rooms that are most relevant. Websites having keywords that are more identifiable and relevant tend to get more than one room; this means that the more famous a keyword is, the larger the bedroom, and also, more people will be accommodated in it.

Search engines use many small databases that are based on keywords instead of using one big database containing everything. This makes some sense; just the same way products are listed in a supermarket, making it very easy for customers to find.

When making use of keywords, it's very important for you to go for one that is more specific; this will increase your chances of appearing higher in search results anytime someone types in a query. Even websites that are popular and established having a very wide user base have issues when trying to stay on top with the general keywords.

Structures of the URL

URL, although it isn't seen as important as before, it can affect the rankings of websites in different ways as well as ways in the experience of users while using a website. The first rule is, as users look at your URL, they can predict the type of content correctly to be found on your website, and in most cases, they get it right. A URL having lots of stated parameters and cryptic text or numbers seems unfriendly and intimidating to the users. This is one reason why

URLs having odd wordings, having few recognizable and relevant words must be avoided.

Another point here is to ensure your website's URL is kept very short, not just meant for the main page, but should also go for other pages that are spread out from the main page. This makes it very easy for users to copy and paste or type your website URL into emails, forums, social media sites, blogs, etc.

Third, do well to include in your URL, any relevant keywords from your website as this can go a long way in gaining the popularity and trust of users and can improve your rankings substantially. Note that it could be dangerous, including so many keywords possible in your URL as it could fight against the purpose of doing that.

CHAPTER FOUR

Keyword Research

As discussed earlier concerning the significance of keywords and the important role it plays in search engine optimization. A website can only be optimized relating to the keywords, that if it makes use of the right ones. Keywords can only be put in the right places if you've done a good job by coming up with the most beneficial keywords for rankings as well as those relevant to your content.

Searching for better keywords is not a one-time task, rather it is a continuous process as well as a challenge since the preferences of users, online environments, what's popular or trending, as well as the manner in which people discuss about things, continues to change.

Keyword Research: What Does this Mean?

To discover the best keywords that rank and remain in the trend loop, something is performed by keyword professionals, which is referred to as keyword research.

Keyword research has to do with exploring the terms used by users in queries on search engines, so as to discover keywords for a specific niche that are less competitive, and then these keywords are then analyzed further to discover substitutable or resembling keywords. This endeavor is engineered by keyword research tools that have in-built word suggestions as well as the thesaurus function.

Search engines also have their personal keyword research tools that are made available for webmasters, tools that also give keyword statistics, as in the number of times a particular keyword has been searched and other words that were mostly used with it. Google and Bing have their own tools: Keyword Planner and Bing Keyword Research, respectively. With these tools, webmasters will easily explore tools developed by similar companies which will be of assistance in exploring:

- How competitive the keyword you're about to use is

- The estimated amount of traffic to be generated by these keywords

- Suggestions of keywords to give you similar phrases and new ideas that can be used on a website

Additionally, it is possible to:

- Make use of keyword filters to help in customizing the search

- Add language or location to make use of the targeting feature

- Select the custom date range

- Make use of a negative keyword that won't be included in the research

The major idea behind this activity is to choose keywords that are relevant to your content and will fulfill a website's SEO objectives.

Phases Involved in Keyword Research

There are different phases involved in keyword research, which will help in the development of the final keyword list:

- Identify those keywords that are most relevant to your business

- Include words to change them into more specific keyword phrases (you can include location, adjectives, etc.)

- Check through your competitors' keywords to help you get some ideas.

- Making use of the keyword research tool, check how competitive these keywords and phrases are.

- Get more keyword ideas using keyword research tools

- Get rid of very competitive keywords and generic keywords

- Complete this list with ten to fifty keywords as well as keyword phrases that could be later used in optimizing your website.

The main aim behind keyword research is to get a sort of library of terms that are relevant to a website's content but are yet to be widely used by other webmasters and SEOs. Ideally, keyword researchers are searching for terms having a lesser competition as well as more search potential.

However, a dilemma comes with keyword research. Though terms having little competition are usually very easy to work with when we talk of rankings, they are also characterized by fewer searches as well. Keywords having strong competition may have millions of searches, and therefore there'll be lots of traffic to deliver, but working with it becomes very difficult when it comes to increasing their rankings. Therefore, SEO professionals will make use of different strategies in the type of keywords to pursue as well as ways of pursuing them.

Let us consider what keyword research entails. Let's consider the very popular keywords having a lot of traffic and searches to offer already. First, we'll look at 'weight loss,' which delivers over 14 million results when searched on Google. Now, it is almost impossible to get an average ranking for this keyword, talk more of being ranked on the first page. Now, what a keyword researcher will do, is to find a term conveying the same or similar meaning as 'weight loss' and will also face less battle to rank for this keyword. Let's say we change this keyword to 'voila,' we will have just over 2 million results compared to the over 14 million results of 'weight loss'; this means we have successfully reduced the competition by about 6 times, just by altering these words a little.

Now, more adjustments can be made to this keyword by reducing competitiveness even more by including more keywords to make them more specific. This can be done in different ways, for instance, including a geographical filter by including a country or city to the keyword and then turning it into a phrase.

Let's take a look at another example, which is even more popular compared to the former: 'save fuel,' which gives over 280 million results. Now, you may start thinking of the difficulty in working with this figure. But with keyword research, it is possible. Now, let's replace the word 'save' by another verb that is less common and then replace fuel as well with a less general noun. If you type in conserve petrol, you see that there are just about 370,000 results compared to the initial 280 million. This shows the strength of keyword research. Now let's consider those tools that offer keyword research.

Tools for Keyword Research: Paid and Free

Researching keywords have to do with making use of different tools available online. There are some that can be used for free, while others will have to be paid for. And sure, you'll get some free tools, but you'll only be limited to a very few of its capacities and functions, and will require you to purchase a premium package to have access to the full functions. Here, we'll be talking about some of the most important tools available out there presently, and how best you can use them.

First of all, let's consider the paid tools and what they have to offer.

- **Keyword Analysis by Moz**

This tool allows users to search for 20 keywords with respect to the difficulty of the keyword, the number of times these keywords are searched for every month, and the best 10 ranked websites. If you are a premium member which costs $99, this tool is added to the package. It comes with a free trial for 30 days.

- **Advanced Web Ranking**

This also comes with a lifetime license of $99 but includes the functionality of basic keyword research. Users can have access to the complete features and capabilities of the tool with access to its advanced research functions at $399. Though, considering the cost, this tool is worth it in some areas. It needed, it can provide users with data from 7Search, Google Trends, API related keyword search, Yahoo!, Google Suggest, SEMRush, Wordtracker, Google Webmaster API, and Google Adwords altogether in just one tool.

- **Raven Tools Research Central**

The Raven Tools Research Central offers data from Majestic SEO, SEOMoz, and OpenCalais, with all three in just one location. Just like that of Moz, it features the premium membership of the Raven Tools, which starts at $99 and then includes a free trial for 30 days.

- **Keyword Spy**

The keyword spy is more of an espionage weapon, just like its name suggests. It is more of a tool that counters those competitors and helps look at what is happening backstage. Research can be conducted concerning the organic results, paid results, as well as affiliate keywords that are used by your competitors. This sets you back at $89, which is just the beginning cost.

- **Wordtracker**

Wordtracker is a special tool due to a feature that may not be found elsewhere. It reveals to you what users are typing into their searches anytime they want to purchase something. It presents before you those keywords that are profitable and high performing to meet your e-commerce requirements. This tools' pricing begins at $27 to be included in the bronze membership, while silver and gold membership goes for $65 and $99, respectively. The bestseller is silver, and in most cases, it is more than enough to meet your research needs.

Now, let's take a look at what is offered for free

- **KeywordEye**

Because a British team was responsible for its development, it utilizes Google UK for research purposes but can be adjusted to Google US as well as different other countries as well as their results. With keyword research, you will be given keyword suggestions, which are ordered by their results, search volumes, or other orders that you want to see, like being ordered by AdWords ranking.

- **SEMrush**

Although this is a paid tool, it has a free version that can handle your research needs; this is why it is included among the free tools. SEMrush does very well in informing you of how great the competition is on any keyword used on Google. It provides you with related or similar terms for those keywords you want to analyze. This could prove very useful in staying current.

- **WordStream Free Keyword Tool**

With more than one trillion terms included in the WordStream Free Keyword Tool's database, it changes the game by assisting you in choosing those keywords that are most lucrative as well as possible long-tail keywords.

- **SEO Book Keyword Tool**

With the SEO Book Keyword Tool, users will have access to search volumes on a daily basis, Google AdWords' cost estimates, links to some other databases, as well as a whole lot of different functions. This tool is powered by the keyword tool or Wordtracker.

- **Bing Keyword Research**

Having a search history of about 6 months, delivering organized data rather than just averages, this research tool helps in exploring those things being searched for on Bing by users.

Now, we've gone through ten examples of both free and paid keyword research tools, and it's possible you have some idea as to why these tools are necessary and how efficient, effective, and pivotal they could be in carrying out SEO affairs in general, most especially keyword research. This doesn't have to do with creativity alone but also involves getting your arsenal or toolbox ready so that every SEO creativity can be used practically with ease.

The Importance of a Keyword

Though tools for keyword research can assist webmasters or site owners in understanding what is being searched for by users in search engines and even present the information in an analytic and organized manner, they cannot help you comprehend the value of these keywords as well as how it contributes to traffic. This has to be done the old way, making use of trial and error hypothesis and analysis.

First of all, there's a need for some brainstorming to come up with some parameters out of some questions. How relevant is a particular keyword? If you perform a search using that same keyword, would you be fine with whatever results found on your page? Income wise, how much does this keyword work for you? Is the traffic generated transforming into some financial gains? If these questions confirm your keyword's value, then you should continue.

Secondly, using different search engines, perform a test on your keyword to know your position in terms of competition and ranking, to give you some idea of what you'll be facing. Keywords bringing in some sponsored results or good advertisements right on the top of results has this fair chance of lucrative potential and possibilities for easy conversion.

Thirdly, using paid advertising like Google AdWords or Bing AdCenter and analyzing the movement of this traffic concerning the conversion of users for your site and generating revenue is a useful practice. Go for that choice regarding Google AdWords and then direct this traffic to your website's most relevant page. Next, is to follow this traffic for about 300 clicks or more, watching the conversion rate closely as well as other information.

Finally, you can use the gathered data in constructing a sketch of a certain keyword's value and what you stand to gain in your present set up. Taking a look at visitors that have visited your website and how many of them generated profits for you, you'll be able to have an estimate of how much every visitor is worth in dollars.

If you successfully attracted 200 visitors, where four of them brought gains of $360 for the website, then the worth of each person of the 200 visitors is $1.8, which is decent enough if you somehow rise to claim the top spot to achieve better impressions, raising the click-through rates within few days. With this, 400 visits daily can be transformed into 1200 to 2000 visits, which means that some fortune can be generated within a year.

Demand for the Keyword and the Long-Tail

It sounds great having to work with keywords that have about 10,000 searches on a daily basis. However, it is strange that even these very popular terms actually compose of a little of the percentages performed, which in some cases accounts for less than 20% of all search traffic. These very important keywords that yield profits and most visits are usually found in the long-tail keywords, which is composed of around 70 to 80% of the whole search traffic.

Speaking realistically, the majority of searches are made up of specific, constructed, and unique phrases composed of two or more keywords. When last did you search for 'dogs' on Google? While there could be keywords that have generated results and have so many searches single-handedly, they are responsible for a small fraction of the search traffic in total. What we mean is that the Internet comprises of countless different phrases and keywords that are searched by a few people, instead of just a small number of keywords that are searched by millions. Actually, juicy traffic can be found in the tail.

Secondly, what is the need to get traffic? Why search for better rankings? This is all about making some profits from those visitors to your site. This process is very easy with traffic discovered in the long tail due to the fact that they already have an idea of what they are searching for.

Considering your own website, you have to think of keywords relating to the long-tail keywords of your own. This decision concerning which of the long-tail keywords and keywords to be optimized is a very important one and will most likely affect the kind and amount of traffic, your website's profitability, and rates of conversion of your website. The different parts of your keyword will bring you different traffic types. Having an SEO target that is diversified is a good practice that will focus on the long-tail, coupled with staying updated on newly-discovered long-tail keywords, which can also optimize content having some share of potential in single keywords.

CHAPTER FIVE

Google Rankings

We already know that Google's algorithms make use of about 200 factors in producing rankings for search results. Google only publicly disclosed a few of these. However, guidelines, resources, and tools are not provided by Google for webmasters to use in pursuing better rankings.

From Google's officially released guidelines and documents, SEO professionals have successfully compiled their speculations, experiences, and observations about the backend of the ranking system of Google.

Factors Affecting the Rankings on Google

Three major aspects of a site have a serious effect on the rankings of search engines. These include the experience of the user, a website's usability, and the website's content. Let us start with the experience of the user as well as the website's usability as they have a close link.

- **User Experience and Usability**

Although this variable doesn't have a direct effect on rankings just like the other variables could, like using keywords, link and site structure, experience of the user, and usability usually has an effect on Google having an intuitive comprehension of your site, which it acquired via studying the behavior of users as well as their interaction with your website, the way linking is performed and learning its self-made artificial intelligence.

Since a website's usability and user experience makes it popular and trusted among the users, Google picks this and interprets that the website in question has much value due to the behavior of users. This can also be referred to as indirect influence, whereby the experience of the third party of one site is affecting the response of a second site towards it.

If the construction of your site was done with users kept in mind, and having the feeling of what it would look like visiting a website of your own and what would be expected from it as a user, and if this website of yours has a structure and content that merits bookmarks, promotes sharing, and ensure users return to the site and provide backlinks including other positive affirmations; search engines will see all these as positive, which will then influence their rankings to make it better.

- **Content**

Content can be referred to as a website's blood and life and all that a website is in. This has a simple formula; your content should be well researched and creative enough and should be presented in an effective and creative way. Now let's take a look at how your content is judged by Google.

After the start of the era of Google as well as the birth and rise of search engines late in the 1990s, it wasn't long for them to see that what indicates the quality of a website is the number and ways that these websites are loved by other websites or in any other context users could easily link to them. Since statistics and time proved this indirect and unofficial voting mechanism to be accurate and helpful gauging the value of a website, it remains a part of the algorithms of Google till today, although somehow, they have managed to attain dizzying complexity. This is a simple principle. If your website is earning links, then it must have something great to offer. Therefore, Google presents a reward due to your popularity.

Another vital mechanism or indicator for judging content is through engagement metrics. Anytime a search is conducted on Google, and then you check or scan through the results, your behavior will be analyzed by Google and then heads back swiftly to the results page, this is noted down, and with lots of searches conducted every day (millions), a large library of data is acquired by Google about the way users have got themselves involved with your site.

To explain better, if a visitor is not satisfied with your content, you've made Google look stupid for delivering a lousy return, and for this, Google will drop your website in the rankings to prevent any more dissatisfaction brought to its clients.

If you're tired of hearing about lizards with long tails and spiders, then you might be interested in this. In 2011, Google brought what we call the Panda Update, which is also referred to as the Farmer, and then changed their algorithms' mechanics and philosophy in a fundamental way that websites initially enjoying higher rankings were dropped down to lower levels overnight and sites that never got to the top page were well placed at top positions.

What really happened is that Google started incorporating more machine learning, which imitates a website's human judgment for overall 'likeability' and user experience of the website. As this Panda Update learned more, it grew more intelligent and now takes many subjective decisions that are usually associated with human beings.

The ranking systems are changed by the Panda Update in fundamental ways due to the fact that it gives a more user-centric nature to rankings, and rather than being based on the search engine as before; it is centered on the experience of the user.

This change in the climate of the SEO world, as well as the newly developed philosophy behind the rankings of search engines, has to be accepted if a webmaster or an SEO is to perform greatly in an Internet environment that keeps evolving. These developments need to be celebrated, because they humanize the SEO affair as a whole, which was too mechanical, irrelevant, and formalized to the perspective of users.

Tips to Improve your Ranking on Google

With more than 200 factors to put into consideration, and trying to do SEO, optimize for Google could be an overwhelming task. First, try to consider those things that have changed and how they did after the birth of Panda happened, and secondly, there's no need to bother yourself about the 200 variables required to rise in Google Rankings or getting to know them. Some factors have more importance compared to others. If you can just stick to the Google guidelines and the most reliable recommendations in the world of SEO, then you should have no problems.

Before we take a look at these tips, one basic principle must be put in mind, and it should be made the foundation of getting higher rankings. There's no amount of optimization done that will get you higher in rankings if great content is not created for users, making use of the most creativity and empathy possible.

Google ranks websites better when the keywords are found at the start of title tags.

Let's say you could pick between two different title tags:

- Organic fragrances ensure harmony with the environment and nature. The only way of knowing this is experiencing it

- Promoting harmony with the environment and nature by utilizing organic fragrances. Harmonizing it is only possible if you can experience it.

As a webmaster, which of this would you prefer? Google will definitely go for the first one due to the fact that it begins with 'organic fragrances,' which is a keyword.

Google ranks lengthy contents better than short ones

Different studies revealed that, generically, web pages were preferred by Google, which has over 1500 words present in its content over those web pages having contents shorter than that.

Google takes the page loading speed very seriously.

This is very important since this is one ranking signal that was publicly announced by Google.

Google usually favors websites having responsive design as well as a different site for mobiles.

With about 50% of traffic from the Internet being generated from mobile devices, websites that are designed to work with the device of users and also load themselves are usually rewarded by Google

Google focuses more on the relevance of the link.

Of recent, an ex-employee of Google said that the new PR is relevancy. Google has started paying more attention to the relevance of the link as a form of value and trust, so you should ensure that websites linking to your site, relates to the same topic as yours.

CHAPTER SIX

Google Panda and Other Updates to the Algorithm

In February 2011, Google started releasing what was to turn into game-changing updates that were designed to remove websites having a high number of low-quality content, black-hat SEOs, as well as any webpage deceiving the algorithm into getting the website an underserved search ranking. Many websites, severely hit regarding their SEO visibility, were websites having farmed contents which were very much dependent on search engines for revenue and traffic, which is most probably the reason why the Panda update was also referred to as 'Farmer.'

Google Panda: The Rise

The update of Google Panda, made lots of headlines, not just in the SEO world, but in Internet publishing generally, getting to the extent of getting rid of websites worth millions of dollars overnight or making them bankrupt, making them have a rethink about the models and practices used by their businesses.

Google wanted to bring back those websites having high quality to the right places and then do away with what they refer to as 'thin' websites that took advantage of the algorithm's loopholes and some clever SEO techniques, but had sub-standard content and had lots of irrelevant and intrusive advertising, brought little or no value to the web and their user interfaces were ugly. Some examples of these websites which Google was hoping to target with its first Panda update are www.hubpages.com and www.ezinearticles.com, among others.

Though Google makes changes to its algorithm regularly, with about 500 to 600 changes yearly, the majority of these changes, if not all were minimal compared to what started in February 2011, and they didn't have much impact on a website's revenue and traffic which were much dependent on Google to survive.

Just two websites out of those affected were allowed to make any type of recovery, while some others slumped in their revenues, traffic, and SEO visibility, and couldn't even get back the position held weeks after the Panda rolled out. After Panda's first update, Google kept on finetuning its algorithm reforms, which began in February 2011. This was achieved by releasing more Panda updates, releasing Panda 4.1 in September 2014, which was the latest. Parallel to the updates of Panda, some other changes were floated by Google regarding its ranking algorithms with the EMD update and the Google Penguin.

Having looked at the revolution's brief history in Internet publishing and SEO caused as a result of the shockwaves of its different updates, let us have a detailed look at what the changes in the algorithm are, and how websites are affected, and what it means for an online business, website owner, or SEO professional.

Understanding Google's Algorithms Evolution

We have taken a look at how Panda appeared on the Internet and the SEO scene where its effects were felt more. Let us now have a detailed discussion of what was changed by Panda and how these algorithm changes really work.

A lot of speculation has existed regarding the nature of the changes as well as the factors that led to that large number of websites losing their SEO visibility. The online publishing community as a whole was involved in the presentation of theories as to what constituted the new algorithms and those elements of the structure SEO strategies, and design of websites were to be used in winning the favor of Google; or in other cases, win back the favor of Google and make a move towards recovery.

Below are some of the factors identified in the changes in the algorithm

Machine-Learning Algorithms and Quality Raters

For some time now, Google has been using a human element in its automated ranking system, which is the utilization of quality raters. These quality raters are hired to staff just to review and rate websites, just by answering some questions, which builds up the trustworthiness, authority, and quality of a website, and gave an aspect that is subjective to the automated and objective technical methodology of having an understanding of websites.

The Quality Raters' input, as well as their answering patterns, were then inputted into an algorithm for machine learning, which can be understood as a type of software or artificial intelligence that is capable of learning and evolving, therefore becoming capable of mimicking the functioning of these human Quality Raters. This was changed in a major way by Google Panda, when it made much use of the machine-learning algorithms, therefore giving the Quality Raters a bigger say in what is considered high quality and that which would not.

Now it is obvious that when questions are directed to Quality Raters such as: Is this website one to be trusted with your credit card details? Especially if these are thin websites or shoddy content-farms like Suite101, Ezinearticles, and HubPages, there'd be a clear answer, which is "no." Also, due to the fact that human beings are very capable of distinguishing trustworthiness/high quality from the marketing stunts/low-quality, as a result of years of subjective reasoning and online experience, the strong link existing between machine-learning algorithms and quality raters, that became very important and prominent due to the Panda Updates, changed things, making it very difficult for content-farms and 'thin' websites to deceive the system. However, this approach has a little downside, which is the subjective nature of the Quality Raters' opinion, which could result in an unexplainable criterion.

Additional Advanced Content Analysis

One great characteristic of the Google Panda update, among others, was doing a human and in-depth analysis of a websites' content with more advanced and wider parameters for rating, making use of topic-modeling algorithms.

Initially, Google would only consider the relevance of content on a page compared to the description in the meta-elements, tags, etc., and with Panda getting into the picture, this topic-modeling algorithms became stocked with the ability of distinguishing between a content's finer elements like the readability of a page, a content's visual attraction, how solid and unique the content was, as well as other factors linked to the content.

Rehashed and Duplicate Content

There are so many situations that can be categorized as content duplication. Let us consider some of these:

- **True duplicates present on the inside**

This is a well-known form of duplicate content, and this could happen even with no clever design from your end. When there is a true duplicate found on the inside, it means there are two website URLs that lead to one particular page. Google will believe that this particular user is only trying to deceive the algorithm and then will penalize that user when he or she doesn't pay any concentration to the structures of the URL. This content should be eliminated immediately.

- **True duplicates present on the outside**

This issue is usually caused as a result of content syndication across different domains, which could be either owned by another person or by you. This could also result in these websites being penalized.

If these other domains are owned by you, then a simple catatonic tag can be used to redirect them to just one preferred URL of yours. However, if the content's properties and domains also belong to another individual, then you'll have to find a way to solve this issue with other webmasters.

Another annoying scenario can be mischief, which is caused by scrapers, or people who scrape content and republish it, leading to content duplication, which could also cause a problem for you. Normally, the solution to this situation is developing a site-authority, and in some very severe parasitic cases, there'll be a need to get takedown notice.

- **Quasi-duplicates present on the inside**

Before the reign of Panda, this could have been something relating to SEO, but if applied today, it will get that website into real trouble. This is how the process works. Imagine you have content that is original and sits properly into a theme such as the Haute Couture Fashion and then uses that keyword on that particular page that talks about your boutique. If a minor change is now made to the page's content, just by including one sentence, it then turns it into a new page having tags and meta-elements showing up in searches, as if the whole page was completely different from the first, what you'll see is a duplicate content exempting just one sentence.

The algorithms of Google might not be that smart in noticing what has happened, but just have it in mind that your website will be penalized as a result of this smart SEO stunt.

When these pages are crawled by Google, it picks up whatever is going on instantly, and as a result, it ranks these pages low. Even you might face more penalties, although it may be a serious task to come up with original and new content for this other page having exactly the same theme as the initial page, remember that being penalized is a much more tedious and arduous affair.

Quasi-Duplicates Present on the Outside

This usually happens when affiliates or partners pick contents or some product pages from your website, which leads to a content that appears to be almost a complete duplicate and the bad news here is that Google will give the same treatment, seeing it as a real duplicate and not very impressed naturally.

Ways of avoiding this content duplication are keeping your pages up to date with fresh content, including a unique and original introduction to each piece of content or product page that was borrowed. One other trick that will also help is by introducing more user-generated content on these pages with just a few pieces more than enough to make Google see reasons that your affiliate page and content are not duplicates.

Websites' Search Pages

Though this is relevant to sites having a considerable size, especially shopping sites, some websites with medium sizes may want to pay some attention to this. There are websites having an in-built search feature where visitors can easily make inquiries concerning the contents of the website, like specific articles, individual product pages, or informational pages. With this, it could lead to internal search pages popping up on the search pages of Google, a phenomenon that Google isn't comfortable with. And what causes this discontent is simple.

Google, as a search engine, is very much interested in providing its users with access to pages that are relevant to their search rather than just providing them with more search pages. Solving this conundrum is quite easy though it could take some time. By making use of the robot.txt option, the spiders can be instructed to desist from indexing these pages and block people from following them.

Too Many Ads on Website

Though initially, Google didn't face any problems with this, things have changed lately with Google viewing these websites as low-quality, which is as a result of the pattern discovered by Google's team, since most of these low-quality websites especially those mentioned earlier had a very high ad ratio, that they even started looking like cheap classified ads.

It is natural when website owners try to make their websites easier to finance and more sustainable, with so many ads they could get. However, Google has started taking the ad ratio into consideration, thinking of ranking websites that have a high quantity of ads low, even if there's a lot of high-quality content present on the site. Take note that Panda hasn't just changed the way algorithms work or just some technicalities, but rather led to reinforcement and a deeper shift in the philosophy of Google, where the users are now in charge of measuring all things, and making the search engines an enterprise that is user-centric. Just the same way users prefer seeing fewer ads; Google loves it as well.

One way to help get around this problem, and one that won't make you lose your advertising revenue and still not get your users angry, is paying more attention to those ads performing well, those bringing in money for you, and shedding those ads that earn less or are not relevant.

A very important lesson to learn from this problem is comprehending that new SEO has nothing to do with the search engine but with the user. If you wish to perform well with search engines, you must perform well with the users, understanding what they really want and what would have been your preferences if you were a user. Getting to the heart of Google is by satisfying your online users. This has to do with the general philosophy behind the Internet world and the changing SEO.

Updates made Since Panda 1.0

February 2011: The Rolling Out of Panda 1.0

The initial act of Panda serves as a great onslaught against websites of the content-farm type having lots of high-quality content, which are mostly contributed by the users.

April 2011: The Rolling Out of Panda 2.0

Panda 2.0 widens the range of the initial update from just US search activity to the search activity of all the English language all over the globe. This update is also the first where data usage from blocked websites is recognized by search engines to affect the ratings. However, just 2 to 3 percent of all the searches were affected by the Panda 2.0 update.

Between May & June 2011: The Appearance of both Panda 2.1 & Panda 2.2

These updates only included minor tweaks from the initial 2.0 update that was released in April and even had a lesser impact on searches. The design of Panda 2.2 was made to fight the problem of scraper websites, forcefully taking the rankings of websites having original content and taking a higher position on SERPs. The simple truth is that Google isn't really pleased with the result.

July 2011: The Release of Panda 2.3

Google revealed that new as well as more effective signals are integrated by Panda 2.3 to help discriminate between low- and high-quality websites. Following this update, there were noticeable changes as some websites had higher increases in rankings than before.

August 2011: The Rolling out of Panda 2.4 (also known as the Language Update)

Panda 2.4 was designed to ensure that algorithms perform better with search results across different languages.

September 2011: The Rolling Out of Panda 2.5

Panda 2.5 leads to great changes in search results relating to the large web outlets. Android.com, Facebook, and Fox News are examples of some websites found at the top when searches are conducted.

November 2011: Panda 3.1 is Rolled Out

This update is a pretty minor one that influences just 1 percent of search activity.

January 2012: The Introduction of January 30 Pack

January 30 Pack is just a cocktail of tweaks in different places to ensure the overall experience of users while using the search engine is improved, improving the convenience of the results, with respect to the cultural and geographical context of the searcher. Included is a unique feature known as Megasitlinks, where Google gives results that are more relevant to a searcher's location.

January 2012: The Introduction of Search+ Your World

Personalization was introduced buy Google into its search activity, including the Google+ profiles and social data to the pages of search results, coupled with a feature that allows the switching on and off of the personalization.

January 2012: The Tolling Out of Panda 3.2

Panda 3.2 was released, and Google says no changes were made to the algorithm. The reason for this update is still not clear to anyone yet.

April 2012: The Release of Penguin

Before the release of Penguin, it has been a major talk in the mouths of many, as the design of this update is made to target over-optimization and spam. This update picks up on several things, such as abusive anchor texts and keyword stuffing.

May 2012: The Rolling out of Penguin 1.1

This update is described as Google as those changes in the algorithms meant to target those sites that fail to meet quality standards and are violating guidelines actively.

June 2012: The Release of Panda 3.7

Some SEO experts have revealed that, in terms of search quality, Panda 3.7 impacts search activity more compared to Penguin. Though Google has downplayed the number and says that just 1% of websites in the United States and globally have been affected.

June 2012: The Silent Release of Panda 3.8

There is no algorithm change in Panda 3.8; the only change here is the data update. There is minimal impact, and it is difficult to identify.

July 2012: The Rolling Out of Panda 3.9

After this update, it seemed like rankings fluctuated for about six days, while it was revealed by Google that about 1% of websites were affected.

August 2012: Seven Results on DMCA and SERPs Action

Major changes were announced by Google this month. First of all, just seven results will be found on the major search page in contrast to the initial top ten. Secondly, websites that were repeat offenders when it comes to copyright violations will be actively penalized by Google, using a tool referred to as DMCA takedown information.

September & October 2012: Overlapping Updates put out by Google (the 20th Panda and the EMD)

EMD, which is referred to as the Exact Match Domain update, was done to target exact match domains. Search engine online watchdogs were finding it very difficult to comprehend if the spikes seen in traffic was caused as a result of the EMD update that was announced or the new Panda update. Shortly after, Google made an announcement that another Panda update has been released and that the SEO community thought it best to end the 3.X naming system and then give it another name – Panda 20, since this as the 20th update to be released. Panda 20 was one of the major updates, with about 3 to 4 percent of search activity being affected, which includes non-English searches.

October 2012: The Silent Release of Penguin 3.

This update – Penguin 3, was a minor one, which affected about 0.3 percent of the search activity made in English.

November 2012: The Release of both Panda 21 and 22

Having a lesser impact compared to Panda 20, about 1.2 percent of search activity based in English was affected by Panda 21. Panda 22 was just an update of data of a minor nature.

December 2012: The Release of Panda 23 around Christmas

Having much impact than the initial updates (Panda 21 & Panda 22), this new Panda 23 affected about 1.3 to 1.4 percent of all searches made in English. Though Google maintained that it was just a refresh.

January 2013: The Release of Panda 24

Google officially announced Panda 24, and immediately, about 1.2 percent of search questions.

March 2013: The Release of Panda 25

Panda 25 was seen as a minor update, and this time, the SEO community and critics in general, started losing patience with the endless updates made by Google, which they must always look out for.

May 2013: The 'Phantom' Algorithm Update

With its full details still unknown coupled with no information yet from Google on changes made in the algorithm, so many websites reported heavy losses during the period when the Phantom update made an appearance.

End of May 2013: The Release of Penguin 2.0 or Penguin 4

Though there was much talk about this new Penguin before its release, after its release, it made a modest impact. The exact details of changes effected by Penguin aren't clear enough, but there's some proof suggesting that it focused more on the page level.

May 2014: Panda 26 (also referred to as 4.0, is released)

Panda 4.o became the update having the highest impact since the first update (Farmer), with its impact having a range between 7.5% of search queries made in English as revealed by official figures and about 9% as revealed by the SEO monitor websites. This update seems like an algorithm update, as well as a data refresh.

July 2014: Flight took by the Pigeon

The Pigeon update was released by Google, which was meant to offer better search result experience locally by creating some kind of link with Google Maps. It has a strong effect on SEOs and business immediately since very strong ties are created between the core and local algorithms, increasing the list of the different signals which have already been used by Google to determine to rank.

September 2014: Panda 4.1 Rolled Out Slowly

The search engine giant revealed that this update was a major one having a very strong algorithmic portion. As predicted by Google, the impact was about 3 to 5 percent of searches made, though these numbers are already becoming understated due to the SEOs coming in and the webmaster's feedback.

Google revealed that this latest Panda update would be the last for a long time, and it was created to achieve wider diversity in results by assisting small as well as medium-sized websites having the high quality to achieve better visibility. Also, it is meant to assist Google in weeding websites having low quality with better precision.

Most SEO experts believe that the Panda update released recently is gentler and more empathetic due to the fact that Google has learned some lessons from the previous update made and have decided to take the complaints and feedback of site owners, bloggers, and webmasters very seriously. But we will see how long it will take, as websites that were wrongly affected during the Panda updates start making some recovery to flourish again.

Now let's go to the final section, where we will be talking about the chaos that came to be from Panda as well as other updates and what this means for SEO professionals, business owners, bloggers, or webmasters.

Staying Safe after the Aftermath of the Panda Updates

The search engine optimization and online publishing world continue to change, and if the new game is not learned and efforts made to stay ahead of the cord, then you may end up losing out and not even having the opportunity to play again.

A Quick Lesson for a New SEO Environment

First, as a webmaster or someone just gifted at creating better relationships and links with search engines, you must realize that your job has changed radically and most probably to take a better direction. You now answer more to the users than what search engines offer, due to the fact that Google itself only ranks websites high just the same way they hold favor with the users.

After these changes are initiated, building stronger and better relationships with these search engines now require building a stronger and better relationship with your online users. Achieving this is only possible by focusing on the user experience.

Ensure that a paradigm shift takes place in your design and work philosophy, an area where you're are striving hard to provide convenience, serve, inform, and entertain users since these happy users are a strong signal that can be sent to any search engine. Chasing links and smart keyword densities aren't just enough these days. You need to move on just the same way that these search engines have.

As a webmaster or SEO professional, you're responsible for:

- Interacting with the users

- Building the community

- User-experience

- Amazing design

- Networking with other blogs or websites

- User related metrics

- Responsive design

- Content having high-quality

So, in a way, you can be called a strategist or web consultant, rather than someone who sits trying to know the number of times a specific keyword needs to appear and how someone can be convinced by you to help you with a link. The SEO horizons have broadened qualitatively and immensely.

Another cognitive and conceptual change that should happen is dismissing the idea or belief that search engines are a wall of code or robotic machinery that needs to be breached. Google has started reinventing itself to give rewards to well-meant and high-quality content that adds lots of value to the web and stays focused on users' needs and experience. If this can be done, then you don't have to worry about being affected by a Panda update or being lost in SERPs.

CHAPTER SEVEN

Link Building

For a very long time, links have led to an unofficial, yet significant democracy on the web, with links having equal value just the same way search engines, see the value held by a website.

The Significance of Link Building

When someone links to your site on their page, search engines interpret it that the website owners are indicating or drawing the attention of Google to the greatness of the website. For example, if Lonelyplanet.com or WIRED magazine links to your site, then it means some sort of endorsement from a celebrity.

Therefore, as a result of being indicators of authority and trust, most especially depending on where this link in question is got from, building links have suddenly become a significant factor among the list of factors responsible for rankings on search engines. This had a great influence that it led to a practice of building links in the SEO world and even included a spammy, notorious, and black-hat SEO techniques like abusing anchor text, link farming, etc. Some webmasters and SEO professionals started using link building in deceptive and manipulative ways to deceive algorithms in thinking that they were more relevant and popular that they actually were.

At this point, Google decided to do something, unleashing so many updates that have affected the SEO community, beginning with Panda, and getting some dominance with Penguin, with the EMD update coming up as the latest. As soon as Google discovered how some black-hat SEOs, as well as some white-hat SEOs, were abusing link building, and the ways in which linking has turned to rig the algorithm so as to create a wrong impression of how important, popular, or trusted your website is, it then swung into action to ensure webmasters and SEOs focus more on organically-deserving links due to content and a committed and diverse user base.

Since this paradigm shift came to be, as well as penalties given to those not sticking to the set guidelines by search engines, the building of links have fundamentally changed, in both its practices and philosophy. This new paradigm, as encouraged by Google and ensured by new algorithm filters such as the Penguin update has already transformed the SEO world, as well as the ways we think when optimizing. White-hat SEOs are now seen as the new black-hat SEOs. It is best to get ahead in this curve and accept the changes going on in the online environment.

Links make up of a very important source to gain traction, attention, and traffic from the search engines, most especially if relationships are being built with well-known sites having link partners with trust and authority. Therefore, for SEO professionals, the building of links is a very important task when we talk about pursuing satisfactory traffic and search engine ranking. You cannot comprehend the significance of link building is you don't learn what the concept is all about. So, let's take some time to learn what link building is all about.

Types of Links

SEO professionals, in the future, will probably understand how their field came to be like the era that came before Penguin and the start of the era after the update of Penguin. The reason for this claim seems to be getting obvious today, with so many websites as well as some popular SEO companies heavily penalized by the search engines, leading to their strategies for link building turning negatively against them.

There has been a fundamental change in the game, and unless you have an idea of what it is today, you shouldn't just be expecting failure, but getting some punishment by search engines; this could take a lot of effort and time to recover from. This has become a big reason to worry for webmasters and SEO professionals, who, in the past, tried out different techniques to get higher rankings and had nothing to lose. Now, for everyone seeking to optimize, setting off new algorithms, and avoiding penalties is a major priority.

Take note that it has to do with quality now. In the past, SEOs may have successfully passed off websites and contents of low-quality having smart link building strategies and techniques; however, this period seems to be over or is drawing closer to that. Here we'll be looking at links that should be built, those to be avoided unless you are clever enough to pull them off, and those links you must avoid completely.

Natural Links (or Editorial links)

These types of links are what all SEO aspires to and usually results in real optimization. Natural or editorial links have to do with links made by other people on their own to your website. The word editorial is being used because this was done out of their choice.

These types of links are loved by Google, and this is so because they take hard work and time. At least, you should give a very important reason as to why a webmaster, blogger, or an influential and popular website, why they have to link to you. An example of a good reason to find your way onto other websites and blogs is that you have unique content that no one has or has ever shared.

Manual Links (or outreach links)

These are links expected to be given to websites by SEOs. The building of links manually has to do with contacting blog writers or website owners and making a request to them to be linked to their blogs or websites. Today, there'll be a need to deliver some reasoning, and, on your part, there'll be a need for some convincing. It will be much easier convincing people that have to do with your field.

Self-Promotional Links (or non-editorial links)

These relate to the outcasts of the world of links and are suddenly becoming so, and this comes with a very good reason. Though, before the era of Penguin, so many people did some link building making use of this technology due to the fact that algorithms could be conned into thinking content is relevant when in the real sense, it isn't. But beware, Google has advanced its methods, and these types of links do not just have any value, but they can also trip up filters in the algorithms, which will lead to you being heavily penalized by the search engine. Although they shouldn't be used at all, if you discover that it will be difficult working without them, then ensure that you make use of locations that are not moderated, whether they are forums, comment sections, or directories.

Beginning a Link Building Campaign

Just like other campaigns, it begins with determining the campaign's goals or objectives. Remember that though you're doing something referred to as link building, you're definitely involved in a type of online marketing, which usually begins with some goals or objectives. Your objectives have to be relevant and realistic. When we talk of a realistic meaning, we mean it has to be achieved in a specific time frame with resources already possessed by you.

Relevant means link building shouldn't be a goal but should lead to achieving more progress or success for any individual, organization, or business you are promoting. For instance, get about 15 well-known blows and then getting links from them seems like a great goal; however, will this goal affect the growth of your organization or business? Is the content ready to convert your new traffic into customers or users, or to form a strong relationship with your new visitors? Take, for instance, in the first week, you had 200 new visitors, but as at that time, your website had no contents, and the majority of these visitors left disappointed and unimpressed. In the bigger picture, was your goal achieved? Actually, it caused some harm, because it's possible that the majority of these users will not even visit your website again even after the contents of the website is improved because they will remember the past disappointment.

So, the best way to start out right is setting objectives, because if this isn't done, anything done after without this could be resources, time, and effort spent in the wrong way; a way which could even cause you some harm.

Lastly, keep in mind that though link building has to do with online marketing, in the time frame of its results, it is different; this is because it won't be instantaneous compared to putting up a television channel or an online advertisement. This doesn't say that it is a failed campaign. You shouldn't promise immediate results for any blog or website you're doing link building for.

What Are Your Assets?

Just like barter back then, if you'll get links from others, there's a need to have something to trade with these people as well. This is why website owners or bloggers would care about what you have to offer; something attractive enough for them to put a link up for you. This reason is what we refer to as an asset, and this differs for different websites, and also depends on whether you're an individual, organization, or business. Assets have to be relevant to those people you wish to attract. Some examples of what an asset is are:

- Services

- Community

- Products

- Content

- Data

Lastly, you must keep it in mind that money is not what can be offered in link building. Though, some may say it was never a preferable one to start with. Individuals, websites, and SEOs involved in purchasing links are actively penalized by Google.

Links Exist In Many flavors

The next thing to do is plan the type of links needed by you and the sort of mixture. With link building, you are opportune to utilize different types of linking depending on the campaign needs. From deep links that have to do with making deep links to pages within the structure of a site, to a content piece or a specific product, to brand-linking, which has to do with the creation of links containing your company name or brand information. After having a full analysis of your link profile and website, you can decide on a special sketch of your needs and requirements. Search for areas of innovation and improvement. Below are some types of linking you can choose from:

- Brand linking

- Deep linking

- Links containing target keywords

- Links to your main page/homepage

Building a campaign with the help of a linking strategy to achieve great results, as well as a better link profile, is very good.

Social Links

We can't talk about the types of links, without mentioning social links. These links are obtained from social networks. Although they may not be as powerful and relevant as links that are posted on some other websites, it is seen that social links have some value when determining to rank, as they can reveal the quality possessed by a particular page. If any page is shared multiple times on social networks, then it is offering some value, which usually indicates original or high-quality content.

This is one reason why marketing using social media has turned into an integral part of online marketing; therefore, it can be linked to SEO (Search Engine Optimization). Asides being available on social media as well as engaging with your users and followers, one other method that aids social sharing from your site or blog directly is making use of the social sharing buttons; this can be installed on your website as a plug-in.

Searching for your People

Now that you're set, then you'll have to consider those people you'll reach out to for links and form a link partnership with them. You must ensure that whosoever you'll be contacting will have some interest in the type of content you're creating since the random contact of people could result in a low response rate, which could then result in a lower success ratio.

One way of ensuring better responses is placing some 'hooks' in your pieces. Hooks are what get the interest of potential linkers or makes them committed to considering your content, which is an important element that ensures viewers stay put, wanting them to go through what you have for them. Below are some examples of hooks:

- Ego-bait

- Interesting news

- Competition

- Data visualization

- Controversial/Brazen/Edgy

- Audiovisual content

- Humor/Funny

Just like LinkedIn or Facebook, social media websites are nice places to get an idea of how people spend their time on the web and what is being shared with others. Patterns in the contents to be passed on should be identified, and these elements should be worked on into hooks, which is placed in your content.

Once you've been able to gather a list of people that could possibly want to link to your site, then this list can be searched on any search engine. For example, if one potential linker targeted by you is a blogger that deals in travel contents, then using a special tool i.e., Chrome Scraper plug-in, a list of travel blogs can be searched for to get those URLs which is copied from the results page all at once, then this is pasted into a spreadsheet or to an email's working page.

Tools such as the URL Opener will open all the websites all at once. Search for any contact information on the website, either a Facebook Page, a LinkedIn account, Twitter, email address, etc.

Using tools such as Followerwonk allows users to search the bios and accounts of Twitter for your desired keywords. So, if your site is about pipes and cigars, delivering reviews and products, then it will be great searching for keywords like pipe enthusiast or cigar aficionado with blogger or just cigar blogger and tobacco blogger to reach those people having a Twitter accounts and websites that relates to your content. These results can then be downloaded into a spreadsheet.

The next thing is to discover much about your potential link partners to help you compose a personalized and relevant message. Emails resembling automated messages shouldn't be sent out. Consider this as a person's SEO instead of a search engine. You'll definitely want every person out there to really like you if you want your list to be very successful.

It is also great that during your outreach, the link targets should be sorted in order of preference in terms of the Domain or Page Authority they possess. Secondly, sorting can also be done based on the number of followers they have on their social media accounts. Lastly, giving priority may have to do with how they relate to your field.

Your target's minimum Page Authority should be 1, while for Domain Authority, it should be 25. Depending on the length of your list, these values could be [higher or lower. Make use of the MozBar tool to help you determine a website's Domain and Page Authority.

Also, extreme caution has to be taken when making use of generic greetings like 'Dear Blogger' or 'Hi Webmaster.' They might feel your email is another automated spam that they usually receive.

A good message should be composed of the following:

- The name of the other person

- Disclosing your current location

- A specific or detailed comment about their job

- Having a very good subject line

- The email signature used by you should be authentic

It is also advisable not to use any famous free email from either Google or Yahoo! because they are usually used by spammers. Lastly, ensure you follow up with those website owners and bloggers you're targeting, because they probably get lots of emails, 'which makes it very difficult for them to go through all. Also, don't allow yourself to be weighed down with negative responses; just request feedback for your content. Some of the bloggers may dislike your present content, but they may like something else later in the future.

Tactics for Link Building

Links can be found in more than one way. Different methods exist. There's a need to get some tactics that will work for your SEO context. We have industries or fields that tend to lean more towards aggressive link building, focusing more on getting rid of competition, while some others will be more focused on building a network of forums and blogs with developers having a similar mindset. Whatever your needs and requirements for building links are, let's consider the different link tactics that are applicable for different online contexts.

Content-Based Linking

The importance of content-based linking is making efforts to get links by developing assets, which basically are different contents. Let's consider what this could be:

- Videos

- An infographic

- A how-to guide

- An image gallery

- Data visualization

It's better to write content that turns into an asset for you, while considering your target link partners – those that see your asset (content) as attractive due to the fact that it is thrilling, interesting, informative, funny, etc. The most important of all is that they should see it important and relevant to their websites, blogs, or what and who they represent as Internet community members. You then contact these people and try to convince them, so they link to your website.

Eventually, you'll prefer a place where each link acquired won't be a link you requested, but rather given links by well-known community members that can influence others and then assist you in gaining their popularity. Though this is a strategy (long-term) that requires high-quality content, this is possible.

Guest Blogging

This is the practice of contacting other website owners or bloggers to know if they'll be publishing your content. Though in a technical sense it is not illicit and this could be a very good way of acquiring links from reliable sources, some marketers and SEOs used this tactic the wrong way and used contents that were below standard coupled with anchor texts that are spammy, which forced Google to punish those behind the abuse of guest blogging.

Broken Link Building

Sometimes, fixing broken things comes easier compared to the building of new ones to replace them. Broken link building follows the principle mentioned above. There are fairly abundant broken links in the World Wide Web, and any SEO professional that is smart enough should see an opportunity in cases where others are seeing ruins of a once-great link. As broken link building has now become many people's favorite link building tactic, which works by identifying those broken links present on the web and rendering help to webmasters that are troubled by replacing these links with better ones that benefit them.

Most broken links are usually found on high-quality websites, so getting a chance for a broken link to be fixed in your favor is just like getting a gift.

Generally, the itinerary of any building exercise regarding broken links will look like this:

- Find broken links and then identify those targets of value

- Contents created should impress the webmaster

- Conduct outreach and then just sit back and enjoy the free link.

To develop the skills of your broken link building better, search for resources online to bail you out. There are a whole lot of them out there.

CHAPTER EIGHT

Search Engine Services and Tools for Webmasters

A sides that the SEO community is actively involved in the creation and innovation of more tools to be used by organizations, businesses, and SEO professionals seeking to self-optimize, so many different services and tools are made available by search engines to assist webmasters during their SEO endeavors. For example, Google has different tools, advisory, and analytics content that is specially designed for webmasters searching for ways to have a stronger relationship with the search engine and that their websites are optimized in line with the recommendations of Google. After all, who can understand search engine optimization far more than the search engines?

Search Engine Protocols

Let us consider the different search engine protocols out there:

Robots Exclusion Protocol

The functions of this protocol are possible via the robots.txt file that is normally found in a website's root delivery. This protocol gives directives to automated spiders and web crawlers concerning the different issues like guiding bots as to where sitemap data can be found, the different areas of a site that are disallowed or off-limits, and shouldn't be crawled, and parameters given for crawl delay.

Below are the commands that could be used in instructing the robots:

Disallow: This prevents the robots from coming close to some folders or pages on a given website.

Crawl-delay: Crawl-delay provides the rate at which robots crawl pages on a given server.

Sitemap: With this command, robots will easily locate the sitemap as well as other files related to it.

Beware: While the vast majority of robots are compliant and nice, there are some of them whose design doesn't work in line with the protocol and therefore, will not follow the directives presently in the robots.txt files. These robots, at any time, could be used by dubious individuals to access the content they shouldn't have access to or steal private information. To prevent this from happening, the best move is to leave the administrative sections' address in the robots.txt file.

Also, you can use the Meta robots tag for these pages in order to inform these search engines not to crawl the pages. To analyze and access your website's search engine protocols, you can make use of the Google Webmaster tools.

Sitemap

A sitemap can be seen as a treasure map that leads search engines through the right path to crawl your website. With a sitemap, search engines are assisted in finding as well as classifying the contents found on a website, which could have been difficult locating on a normal day. There are different formats used in keeping sitemaps in. They can also reveal ways to different content forms, whether they are news, mobile, or audio-visual version files.

A tool referred to as XML-Sitemaps.com is used in creating sitemaps in an easy and friendly manner. Sitemaps come in three major formats:

- **RSS**

There has been a serious debate concerning if RSS should stand for Rich Site Summary or Really Simple Syndication. In terms of maintenance, it is quite convenient and can be coded, so they take on automated update properties coupled with the inclusion of new content. One downside of the RSS is that it is difficult to manage compared to other formats.

- **XML**

XML refers to Extendable Markup Language. When it was being created, someone decided that the XML sounds better compared to EML; this is how the initials got stuck. Most website design gurus and search engines recommend the XML format, and it's not surprising to see that it is also the most widely used. Being more passable by the majority of search engines, it is easily created by many different sitemap generators. Also, you'll have the best control of a page's parameters.

However, one disadvantage of this format is that the file sizes for these formats are usually heavy compared to some other formats.

- **TXT File**

This format seems to be very easy to use, and for each line, it makes use of one URL and can go up to about 5,000 lines. The downside here is that it doesn't allow Meta elements to be added to pages.

Meta Bots

Meta bots can be used in giving instructions to search engine robots pertaining to just one page at once. This tag is usually included in the HTML file's head area.

The Nofollow attribute

As mentioned earlier, nofollow links help you link to a particular page without having to go through any linkjuice. Though search engines will stick to your wishes not to give any value to these links, they may end up following them for discovery reasons.

The Canonical Tag

You can end up with different URLs that cause similar pages of similar content. This may not be a big deal, but the repercussions are unhelpful for SEOs and site owners looking to enhance page value and ratings. This is because the search engines are yet to be very smart as we would want them to be.

This tag is used to inform search engines about which to count as 'authoritative' for result purposes. This helps sear4ch engines to comprehend all the versions of a specific page, and just one URL should be counted for the purpose of ranking while others have to be assimilated into it.

Myths and Misconceptions of Search Engines

Honestly speaking, we've all somehow heard of SEO legends, and even after being proved untrue and debunked, it still fills our minds with doubts. Below is a collection that may be of help in separating facts from fallacies.

Making Use of Keywords

This can be referred to as one of the most persistent and oldest fallacies of the world of SEO, and it seems invincible. This hidden truth of this SEO technique is that stocking anchor text, title, a page, and content with so many keywords is a special way of getting to the top of search engines. Sadly, so many SEOs still believe it to be true, and so many SEO tools stress the significance of the density of keywords and how they are used by the search engine algorithms. We are saying that this is false.

Keywords used with moderation, intelligence, and relevance are usually admired by search engines. Time shouldn't be wasted on the calculation of mathematical formulae as well as counting of keywords. Doing this will only annoy visitors and then make you look like a spammer.

Using Paid Results to Improve Organic Results

This can be called pure fiction. This never happened, and it is still not going to happen. Even countries that may be spending millions of dollars in search engine advertising may still need to fight or struggle over organic results, and no extra support is received by them or the slightest change in rankings when we talk of organic results, even when paid results are used.

Bing, Yahoo, and Google all have a strong separation between the departments to protect this type of crossover from happening and then risk the legitimate nature of the search engine machinery as a whole. If any SEO says he can do some magic regarding this, then get ready to take to your heels and run.

The Myths of Metatags

We quite agree that, thus, used to true and worked effectively for a short time period, but for a considerable time period, it has failed to be included among the ranking's equation. Many years ago, search engines used to permit users to utilize the meta keyword tag while inserting relevant keywords from your content so that anytime the keywords of a user somehow match with yours, you would also come out automatically in the query.

However, the same category of people that played a role in the rise of the first myth utilized this method of SEO to the spamming overdose limit, and it wasn't long for search engines to regret whatever they did and get rid of this method from its algorithms. Therefore, be warned now, because this method has stopped working. Those referring to SEO as Meta tagging are obviously still existing in the previous decade.

The Measurement and Tracking of Success

We've seen this as a universal management rule that anything that can be measured can also be changed. Though this doesn't hold true in all cases, it applies to the search engine optimization field. SEOs that are successful are known to use strong tracking and make use of measurement, which plays a significant role in success as well as the creation of better strategies.

Below are some of the metrics you'll want to track and measure regularly:

Traffic from Search Engines

It is important to know the source of traffic that has contributed the largest share of traffic on your website every month. These sources are classified into four major groups which are based on the origin of the traffic:

- **Direct navigation**

These set of people typed in your website's URL and then came across your homepage, or those that have saved your website on their bookmarks, or those that were referred to your site by a friend on email or chat. Email referrals cannot be tracked.

- **Referral traffic**

This type of traffic refers to those visitors that came to your site after coming across some promotional content from links that are found all over the website or through some campaigns. These can easily be tracked.

- **Search engine traffic (referred to as organic reach)**

This refers to the query traffic sent by the search engines due to the searches made that show your website on the results page, and then the user visits your URL by visiting the link on the results page.

- **Social traffic**

This traffic has to do with the visits that come from social networks, which permits website owners to measure those benefits yielded by your efforts on the different social media platforms regarding visits and conversions.

Having some knowledge about the percentages and figures makes it possible for you to see where your strengths and weaknesses lie, to comprehend your decreases and increases in traffic, and its sources to pick up those performance patterns that may be illegible if you're not considering the larger picture with some segmentation.

Referrals due to some phrases or important keywords

It is very important to know those keywords that bring in the largest traffic, as well as those not performing up to expectations. Your website may be less optimized for keywords that normally should bring in lots of traffic and already contributes greatly to traffic.

Remember that, if your website comes as a song, then the keywords would be what everyone remembers, which will either be the memorable parts of the melody or lyrics. So, it is very important to know those keywords are doing for your website. The website's analytics are not complete without tracking the website's keywords performance on a regular basis. The good thing about it is that there are lots of tools out there that can assist you in keyword metrics.

Referrals by some search engines

It is very important to measure the performance of your website in relation to some search engines, not just the way your website is performing with search engines in general terms. Let's consider some reasons why having a picture of your relationship with some search engines is important:

- **Comparing the share of the market against performance**

This makes it possible for the traffic contribution of some search engines to be analyzed in line with their share of the market. Different search engines perform well in different fields of search categories. For instance, Google performs well in better areas characterizing more technology, Internet-literate, and younger population, in contrast to some other fields such as sports or history.

- **Comprehending visibility graphs data**

In the event of going into search traffic, if separate measurements can be kept of exact and relative contributions from some search engines, then it places you in a bigger and better position to locate where the problem lies. For instance, if there's a drop in the traffic and it is consistent across different search engines, then accessibility may probably be the issue rather than one having to do with penalties, where there'll be a larger drop in the contribution of Google compared to the others.

- **Inquiring into strategic worth**

Since some search engines respond in a different manner to optimization efforts, it is very easy to have a strategy that is focused and more effective in play, if it's possible to identify which optimization tactics or techniques are doing well for the search engine. E.g., keyword-centered methods and on-page optimization deliver results that are more significant on Yahoo! and Bing compared to Google. So you'll have an idea of what needs to be done to increase your rankings and attract some traffic from search engines and what might have been done the wrong way.

SEO Tools

Asides those tools mentioned earlier; several other tools can be mentioned as well, as they could assist website owners with different tasks regarding SEO, as well as measuring how your strategy came out successful.

The most significant of these tools are from Google – Google Webmaster tools (Bing has a similar tool designed those webmasters seeking to optimize websites for Yahoo! and Bing) and Google Analytics.

The main advantages of these tools are:

- This tool has a free version, which means anyone is allowed to make use of them. You only need a Google Account.

- It is easy to navigate, and therefore, even as a beginner, you'll have no problems making use of them

- They offer data that assists you with improvement in the usability of the website

- You'll have the opportunity to link to other services rendered by Google, like Google Ad Words, to help create a comprehensive report to improve and analyze the strategy's performance.

Webmaster Tools

All webmasters should have this tool because it helps in analyzing and tracking a website's overall performance, structured data, crawl errors, internal links, etc. With your Google account, this webmaster tools can be accessed for free. Your website will have to be added to your Google Webmaster account to help you retrieve this information about your website.

Furthermore, this Google tool gives viable suggestions regarding your website's improvement concerning HTML improvements, which is very helpful when we talk of website optimization.

Some HTML improvements are:

- • Missing title tag

- Missing meta description

- Too short or too long meta description

- Duplicate title tag

- Contents that cannot be indexed

- Duplicate meta description

- Too short or too long title tag

Google Analytics

This tool can be used in tracking a website's performance, visitors' behavior, sources of traffic, etc. Google Analytics delivers much data about your site, which can assist greatly in learning about those visiting your site (your audience), the ways in which they arrived at your site (acquisition), their manner of interaction (behavior), as well as the time spent by these visitors to your website. The activity can also be monitored in real-time and the conversions analyzed by linking to Google AdWords or setting up goals.

PageSpeed Insights

Since a website's loading time is a very significant factor affecting rankings, you should know about the speed of your website and make efforts to improve it.

When your website URL is analyzed, you'll get some suggestions that relate to the optimization of your website's different parts, which affects the speed of the website. These are:

- Image optimization

- Response time of the server

- Avoid redirects

- Prioritizing of visible content.

- Enables compressions

- Browser caching

- Gets rid of CSS or render-blocking JavaScript

This tool also offers suggestions on the best way to fix the elements.

CHAPTER NINE

Steps Involved in Website Optimization

Now, you have gained much knowledge about search engine optimization and how websites are ranked and indexed by search engines, you should now learn about ways in which a website can be optimized so as to maximize those chances of you getting a high organic ranking.

Some tasks will be revealed shortly, which will go a long way in achieving this. These tasks are ordered, so you should follow the process while optimizing your website.

The optimization tasks here will be grouped into two. The first category of tasks will have to be completed even before the creation of the website; this means that this stage is meant for those planning to create their websites.

If you own a website already, then you should just focus on the second group to help you optimize your existing website.

Before Creating your Website

Research

This area is very vast; this is where the opportunities and possibilities for the creation of a website are explored and then developing a good strategy for your online business. The research phase deals with the following:

Keyword Research

This is an important aspect of online marketing generally, most especially when we talk of paid and SEO advertising, where there's a need to make use of related keywords to help search engines identify your content and then show it on searches related to it.

Demand Research

This is another part of the research that has to do with market analysis. The online market has to be explored to help determine what is needed by people, what is lacking, as this increases the chances that your website will be successful. If you are operating a local business, include your location to conduct a local search and then explore whatever results these search engines give.

Competitor Research

This phase is composed of two parts. First of all, find out about your competitors. Use search engines to help you discover search pages that come up anytime the keyword found relevant to your content is searched for. With this, you'll easily discover those websites that are trying to rank for the same keywords as yours. Compile these websites, as it could be very useful as time goes on when the need arises to monitor these competitors and then comparing the progress they have made with yours.

Once these competitors are known, try to perform an analysis of their websites, as this could help you know what things they do well, and those things they do wrong. One great tool to assist you here is the Open Site Explorer, which helps website owners to analyze the different aspects of their site as well as help in comparing different websites.

If you own a website already, and you wish to compare it with that of your competitors, then you can use the "Compare Link Metrics" option, which is available in this tool.

Pick a Domain Name

Your domain name must be chosen very carefully, as this will be the name known for your web practices, and it should be very easy for visitors to remember, to help them find you. A name that is easy to remember and short will also be a smart move, especially if this name will be featured on posters, business cards, and flyers.

Pick a Design that is SEO Friendly

We've discussed earlier what an SEO friendly design is. It is a design that lets search engines index and crawl a website very easily. Generally, it is recommended that much attention is paid here, as your website's destiny is largely based on treatments received by your site from search engines. Therefore, you need to make things very easy for search engine crawlers to help them promote your site via organic search results.

Designs that are friendly have to do with a website's design and the URLs that are friendly, as both play a role in ensuring that a website is well-optimized so that it can be well ranked in the results of search engines.

After Creating your Website

After the website has been created, the above guidelines should be followed; then, you're set for the next stage of optimizing your website, which involves different tasks to optimize your website's content so as to maximize the search engine optimization efficiency.

Add Content

Over recent years, content became the focus of online marketing as well as online presence generally. Having contents that are relevant to your website's topic as well as high-quality ones, could go a long way in influencing the positioning of your website.

Unlike what happened in the past, where websites could be easily positioned even without any content, the search engine algorithms evolution has now placed content as a very important metric used when analyzing a website's influence and relevance. This is why many websites today ensure they have a blog as well.

For instance, if what you do is renting bikes, you could include in your website instructions on where and how a bike should be rented. Also, the section regarding your company and contact should be included as well. However, if there's a need to make your SEO better, content that is related to your topic should be considered, which in this case, it is the bike rental.

Today, SEO professionals feature contents via including a blog to the site. Here, articles posted on this blog could focus on biking tours, tires for bikes, advantages of bike rentals, and types of bikes, etc. By doing this, keywords will be used prominently without becoming spam.

The idea behind this approach is that content will be used in increasing your website's positioning by providing original and relevant information. Regardless if we consider the content published on your blog or website, optimizing it is very important so as to ensure its efficiency.

How to Optimize Content

Optimizing your content entails formatting your text so as to help search engines have a better understanding of them, which will also help these search engines in matching your content with keywords that are relevant. Below are some parts of your content that must be optimized:

The Titles

Titles must be catchy, engaging, and interesting, as this attracts and engage the users to read the whole article. Aside from this, the article title has to be related to the article's content, as it will be wrong for you to post titles that are misleading, having nothing relating to the content. Including keywords in your title is recommended as well.

Headings

Your articles must have some headings where the most important aspects of the article will be highlighted. There are two reasons why the use of headings is important. First, an article having headings makes it easier for your visitors to read due to its great structure, and it also lets users scan texts before deciding to read it.

Second, search engines make use of the heading tag and other tags like the title tag to differentiate the different sections of the page of a website. By this, search engines will be able to discover the important information on your site, as the most important parts will be highlighted in the headings. Also, you should try to add keywords in these headings naturally to avoid disrupting the visitors' reading process.

Keywords

Using keywords in your content is another very important part, as you want your site to identify with this. Therefore, aside from making use of keywords in your headings and title, the keywords can also be distributed throughout the text. Asides using exact keywords, you can also use synonyms.

Ensure that these keywords are used naturally. You won't want to repeat the keyword randomly because this will affect the readers negatively; they won't read the whole article, they won't share your post, and will most probably stop coming to your website. This will affect the positioning of your website negatively.

Besides contents that are written, other contents that could be used includes images, infographics, or videos. All these are very important types of content because they focus on making use of visual effects to gain the readers' attention. In addition, presenting your content in this way could be more effective at times compared to writing down the content and publishing it just like an article.

Generally, when optimizing videos, it is advisable that the video's transcript is provided in the article, underneath the video. The majority of users will just watch the video without looking at the transcript; however, since search engines cannot understand the video's content, they'll make use of the transcript's text to index your websites' page.

The images should be optimized as well for this same reason. Images are majorly used in attracting visitors' attention. Aside from presenting a graph or a photo, images could also feature text with the inclusion of an effective message. However, the search engines cannot see any of this, which is the reason why Alt text should be used in describing the image.

Add a Sitemap

We've already stressed how important having a sitemap is, as it makes it possible for search engines to locate any of a website's pages, whether another page is linked to it or not. Below are some cases where it is very necessary to have a sitemap on your site:

- Your website is large and has lots of pages

- Lots of pages present on your site, but they aren't linked

- Few external links present on your website because it's a new one

Integration of Social Media

Another part of website optimization is integrating your social media. The initial part of this integration is letting users share content easily by installing the necessary plug-ins. Plug-ins are usually displayed next to or above the article, which allows the visitors of the website to share your content on their various social media accounts. This happens in just one click, without having to leave your website.

Aside from this, the plug-in reveals the number of times each article was shared on social media, which could encourage visitors to share it.

Aside from integrating the social media plug-ins, you have to be available on different social media platforms. It is recommended that you have accounts on well-known social networks, as this is a great way to connect with social media users.

In fact, with reference to different studies, Internet users today tend to search for information regarding any brand or business via social media, instead of making use of search engines. By this, they can be updated with recent and trending news, sales, and promotion, and these are the major reasons why Internet users will follow your social media accounts.

Having lots of social media followers can also go a long way in reflecting on the performance of your website because you'll have the opportunity to increase the engagement and traffic on your site via social media.

CHAPTER TEN

SEO Recommendations

This chapter discusses the most important SEO recommendations. There are rules guiding Search engine optimization. As a webmaster, you need to understand some important factors required for SEO. There guidelines you need to follow; these guidelines will help your search engines to work well.

For some years now, search engines have existed, and people try to optimize their search engines to get quicker results. As a result of this, some website owners have devised suspicious techniques to make search engines into ranking a website high. There are some ways to detect these suspicious and illegal techniques, and there are penalties for websites caught doing that.

We will be discussing some guidelines that will boost your website's visibility and optimize your site so that search engines can find it easy to index. To avoid getting into trouble, you should abide by the rules and guidelines provided by search engines.

SEO is a technique used to understand how search engines operate so that you can work in line with SEO guidelines, which makes it easy for your website to be easily found by the search engines. As a website owner, you should understand how search engines operate, the process of indexing sites, and how websites' content is indexed.

No matter how engaging, well-researched, and attractive a page is on your website, if you do not optimize your website for the search engines, there are chances that your page will not be visible to search engines, a reason why your page may not be seen in the search results. As a result of this, your website will not generate traffic. On a normal day, your page should generate traffic when users type a topic related to your page.

Whenever you are creating content, the first thing you should think of is search engines, and if readers can understand your website's content structure. Every part of your website, like the menus, blog, home page, etc. should also be considered.

Guidelines for SEO Recommendations

Keep Your Visitors in Mind

Although search engine optimization determines your website's visibility, you have to put your visitors in mind as well. Search engine optimizations are the technical aspect of your content; you need to deliver content that will attract and keep your readers engaged. You should be concerned about how your readers see your content.

Highlight some parts of your text, especially the catchy sentences and main ideas, photos that can pick out the points that are linked to the text, etc. Think about how your visitors will perceive your content when they see it at first. Is your content attractive to your visitors? Will they find it interesting?

Another thing you should also consider is the topic and the introduction of your content. An attractive topic and catchy introduction will keep your visitors glued to your page. The topic of your article attracts your visitors. Therefore, it should be real, engaging, and associated with the content of your website.

With this, your visitors will always want to read your content. Focus more on topics linked to your website; this helps you attract visitors interested in your content. Your visitors will visit your website based on how informative, engaging, and well-researched your topics are.

Stay Updated

Search engine optimization is an aspect of online marketing that keeps changing. Technical advancement fosters the introduction of new techniques, which has a way of affecting your approach to online marketing.

The rapid growth of websites these days is one of the things that affect development. New websites are developed and launched every day, while some sites are shut down, and this keeps affecting the online market because most websites now compete for keywords. This kind of competition can make things better or worse for your business.

You need to keep updated so that you will be able to operate your websites in line with these developments. You need to keep up with the new applications and tools introduced because some tools and applications are handy when carrying out SEO strategy. Different tools or applications are introduced and updated; if you keep up with the trend, you can make effective use of them to improve your website business.

Companies in charge of search engines know about this development, a reason for always improving search engine algorithms. When search engine algorithms are being improved, it helps indexing websites. The goal of these companies is to offer a good user experience; therefore, they have to highlight the best websites only.

Search engine optimization is a process that keeps going. You might need more effort and time to carry out the strategy, and sometimes, you will only need to monitor your website's performance. Ensure you stay updated when it comes to SEO because the techniques in SEO change over time, and these new innovations can improve your website.

Organize your Website Hierarchy

For search engines to crawl and index your content, it needs a URL per content. Different content uses separate URLs so that it can show in search results properly. URLs are divided into several sections. According to Google, all websites should utilize https://.

Your website's hostname is where you host your website. It mostly utilizes the same domain name used for email. According to Google, there is a difference between the "www" and the version that does not use "www."Website owners are advised to add both https:// and https:// versions and also the "non-www" and the "www" versions when including your website to Search Console.

The three parts that determine the content accessed from your server are query string, path, and filename. They are very sensitive. The protocol and hostname are not sensitive to lower- or upper-case letters. A website's navigation plays an important role in helping visitors easily locate the content they need.

Navigation is very vital for search engines as it helps search engines to know the content that is important. When it comes to navigation, plan it based on your homepage. Every website has a homepage, which is frequently visited by readers.

Evaluate your User Behavior and Search Performance

Most search engines offer free tools that webmasters can use to evaluate their performance in their search engine. Google provides a tool known as the Search Console. Search Console answers the following question; how am I fairing in Google search results? Can my content be accessed by Google? Utilizing Search Console can help webmasters identify and address issues that improve their site performances.

Search Console enables webmasters to:

- Evaluate and submit sitemaps

- Identify the parts of a website Google had issues crawling

- Understand how top searches work

- Understand how Googlebot finds pages

- Remove URLs that Googlebot has already crawled

After improving the indexing and crawling of your website with the use of Search Console or some services, you want your website to generate traffic. Web analytics programs such as Google Analytics can help you achieve this. You can use Web analytics programs to:

- Know how users visit and act on your site

- Identify the most read prominent content on your website

- Evaluate how effective the optimizations you did to your website.

For advanced users, analytics programs provide more information about how readers interact with your article. These programs can help you to evaluate how visitors behave on your site and search performance.

Have a Mobile-Friendly Site

We are in the mobile world. These days, most people make use of their mobile devices to search for content on Google. Users may find it difficult to operate the desktop version of your website on a mobile device. Therefore, making your website a mobile-friendly one is important for a good performance.

You should know the difference between mobile devices. Mobile devices include tablets, smartphones, feature phones, and multimedia phones. There are several ways you can make your website a mobile-ready one. After making your website a mobile-friendly one, you can utilize the Mobile-friendly test to evaluate if pages on your website meet the requirements of a mobile-friendly site.

The Search Console Mobile Usability can also be used for fixing issues related to mobile usability. You can use Separate URLs, Responsive web design, and Dynamic serving to make your website a mobile-friendly one. If you are utilizing separate URLs, ensure you test both the desktop and the mobile URLs, so that you can know if the redirect is crawlable.

How to Improve your SEO

Optimize your Images

You can utilize HTML images in your content. The semantic HTML helps crawlers process pictures. You can also use alt text when utilizing a picture as a link. Do not make your alt text too long, and avoid utilizing image links for the navigation of your website.

Ensure you utilize standard picture formats. You can make use of file types that are supported. The majority of browsers support formats like BMP, JPEG, GIF, and PNG. It is very thoughtful to have your filename go in line with the file type.

Alt texts will help search crawlers to understand photos on your website. Adding alt texts to images in your content will help search crawlers to digest the content of your pages easily and also rank among the top in relevant search results.

Do not:

- Use generic filename such as "pic.gif," "image 1.jpg"

- Write too long filenames

- Put keywords in alt text or copy & paste a whole sentence

Improve your user experience

Search engines only reveal information that is relevant and useful, and they reward websites that only offer a good user experience. When we talk about user experience, we mean your website's usability, design, and functionality, among others.

Your website should have not only content but also offer a good user experience. Improving your user experience will enable users to stay longer on your website and find it more interesting because they will know more about your services, business, and products.

When users know more about your website, you are sending a positive signal to Google. If you want your website to generate traffic and rank in search results, ensure that your website uses a nice design.

Improve your Website's Speed

Another recommendation for search engine optimization is speed. Users become more frustrated when it takes a much longer time for a page to open. Some visitors are not patient and, as such, will leave your website. According to a study, if it takes more than 3 seconds for your website to load, about 50 percent of your visitors can leave.

If it takes your website a long time to load, your bounce rates may become high due to this. To enhance conversions on your website, you can improve the speed of your site. According to research, an improvement in your load time will increase the conversions of your website by 7 percent.

Create Unique Content

One of the things that can affect your search engine in a negative way is duplicate content. Google seeks to reward websites having unique content; therefore, they penalize websites not having unique content.

Some contents are not unique because there is a part of your content that is similar to other contents. This could be the fault of your writer. If you found out that your content is not unique, fix the content to make sure that it does not affect your SERP rankings.

You can use plagiarism checkers like Copyscape will help you to identify content that is plagiarized. Make sure you fix these issues immediately; you identify the part of your content that is duplicated. Anytime you add new posts or pages, ensure you check the uniqueness of your content.

Common SEO Mistakes and How to Prevent Them

If you want your website business to grow, you need to follow some guidelines provided by Google. Below are some guidelines that help you to know what is needed to be done and what you should not do.

SEO dos

If you want your website to get better, below are a few things you need to do:

- Create pages for users.

- Create pages with high-quality and attractive content

- Provides users with a map

- Utilize alt tag and title tag to optimize content

- Deliver original and unique contents

SEO don'ts

Below are some actions you should not take if you want your website to get better results in the search engine.

- Avoid using hidden text

- Do not use too many keywords on your page

- Use a considerable amount of links

- Do not include malware to the pages

- Use words wisely

- Create original and unique content

- Do not use dynamic pages because they can be difficult to understand

- Do not use broken links and incorrect HTML

Ensure you follow these do's and don'ts if you want your site to get better. These guidelines will also help you correct some things on your websites.

CHAPTER ELEVEN

The Ultimate Guide on How to Get 500 Visitors and Rank No 1 on the Internet

The requirements of SEO are dynamic; they keep changing over time. It can be quite uneasy to know the latest developments as they keep changing. You must get to know the latest developments if you want to get traffic on your site. If you know what to do, you will get people that will visit your site.

Although some of these requirements are not difficult to meet up with, you just need to keep yourself informed. That is a major reason you need to read this chapter as it keeps you updated on what to do and how you can get 500 visitors. Several factors determine how your site will rank number one on the Internet.

This chapter explains the essential factors that determine SEO ranking; it also sheds more light on how your site can attract 500 visitors.

Over four billion searches are done on Google daily. People do searches on different topics daily. As we all know that information is very important, a lot of people rely on the Internet for their information. One of the challenges website owners face is lack of traffic. It is very discouraging when you own a site that gets very few visitors or none at all.

Website owners do not just create a website for the fun of it; a website is created to give the necessary information required and as well generate profits from it. If you do not get visitors to your site, you can never make a profit. Owning a website is a very lucrative business but can require lots of things. If you do not do these things, you will not be able to determine your sales process.

How to Test and Evaluate the Major Components of your Sales Process

You must test and evaluate the major components of your sales process. As a new website owner, your site might not get traffic immediately; you start, but it is necessary you test the major elements of your sales process.

The first questions that occur to the website owner's mind are: how can I test my website? What exactly am I testing on the Website? It is normal for you to ask these questions because it is something you might not have heard of. There are several things you can test and evaluate on your website, testing these things helps to increase sales.

You can test your website's layout, design, sales copy, etc. If you are a new website owner, you should focus on testing the right elements. The four most important aspects you need to test are:

Order process: This has to be user-friendly so that a novice website user can easily place an order.

Site Navigation: it is used to determine the number of clicks it takes to purchase.

Sales copy: This includes benefits, headlines, and guarantees.

Opt-in offer: it helps you know if you are getting the contact information of your visitors.

You need to test these important components of your sales process before you start thinking of how to get visitors to your site. When you start making sales and have some traffic, you can test other aspects of your website.

Another question that is being asked by people is, how can someone test a website without traffic? If your website is new, it is normal that your website generates no traffic. You can purchase traffic via Pay-per-click search engines. For everyone who makes some searches about the keywords you bid on and clicks via your website, you pay any amount you bid. There are several Pay-Per-Click search engines you can opt for.

Examples of PPC search engines include MIVA, Yahoo Search Marketing, etc. PPC search engines help you to get affordable, qualified, and immediate traffic to your website as long as you bid on some targeted keywords. Not only do PPC search engines provide instant traffic, but they also help your new website to be ranked among the free search engines too.

After some important components of your sales process have been tested, you can start getting traffic for your website on a greater scale.

How Your Website can get 500 Visitors

There is nothing as frustrating as owning a website that generates no traffic. I have heard some new website owners complain about having no visitors at all. It is normal for such to happen, although it could be frustrating. It has been revealed that most website owners quit because of a lack of traffic and not a lack of time.

One of the driving forces of website owners is traffic. When your website gets 500 visitors, you are close to achieving a successful business. Generating huge traffic is very profitable; most website owners find it tasking to get to this level. To get 500 visitors on your website, there are certain things you need to do; these things should not be ignored as they help you achieve your goal of becoming a successful website owner. Below are some strategies that will help you to get 500 visitors:

Focus On Your Content

One of the most important strategies that help you develop your website is your content. The quality of your content is very vital. The content of your post matters a lot; your content sells you. The major reason people visit your website is the content. Great content will attract more people to your website. The most important goal when writing a piece of article is creating helpful, engaging, and good quality content.

The quality of your content matters a lot. Whenever you are writing about a topic, create time to search and write something informative. Search for keywords that are ranking and write more on them. Pay attention to the quantity of your article, not only the quality. Create a piece of content that is at least 2,000 words. Lengthy content is a more detailed and engaging one. Do good research anytime you are writing about a topic. People love well-researched, well-detailed, and engaging content.

Low volume content might not reveal everything your reader needs to know about a topic. Create a good style for your post. Good and creative content will help you get huge traffic for your site. Here are some tips on how to make your article attractive to readers.

- Make your headline powerful: A powerful headline will attract readers to your site. Your headline is your first selling point. Use a headline that will make your readers curious and willing to read your article.

- Make your introduction great: When you create powerful headlines, your readers will be willing to read your article. Powerful headlines will only push your readers to read your article, but a successful post lies in the power of creating an introduction that will make your readers stuck to your post. Make your introduction engaging and highly informative.

- Communicate properly: The major reason you are posting a piece of article is to inform your readers about a topic. Your reader is curious and wants to know about the topic you have writing. Your article is useless if you cannot communicate and carry your readers along. Make use of short and simple sentences. Make your content simple and easy to understand for your readers. You can also share stories to make your article interesting. Avoid creating content that looks clumsy. Make use of bullets and subheadings to break your text.

- Include some tips: Whenever you are creating a post, try as much as possible to provide some tips. Readers love to get some tips that will help them. Your article becomes more informative when you provide tips in your post.

Utilize LSI Keywords

LSI keywords are great ways to generate more traffic on your website. LSI keyword means Latent Semantic Indexing. An LSI keyword is related to the major keyword in your article. The best way search engines can digest the content of a page is through LSI keywords.

In those days, search engines helped to know what a page is all about by just looking at keywords. So, if the word "rental properties management" was found all over your page, then the search engine would realize that your article was about rental property management.

It is a different case today; search engines have been developed to be much smarter than before. The goal of search engines nowadays is to know what the general topic of a page is about. For instance, if your page discusses "how to cook," search engines will look for this keyword and as well as LSI keywords.

You can generate more traffic by using LSI keywords and help to improve your rankings. The question now is, "How do I find LSI keywords?" LSI keywords can be found by searching for LSI on Google or using LSI keyword tools.

How to Use LSI Keywords in Your Content

You now know what LSI keywords are. You should know how to use these keywords in your content properly. LSI keywords can be added anywhere in your content. Below are some few places you can add these keywords:

- Meta description: You can add LSI keywords in your Meta description to make it more attractive. LSI keywords help your Meta description to be more engaging to readers.

- URL: This is another place you can include your LSI keywords. Ensure your URL is not too much and write in simple words.

- Subheading tags: H2, H3, H4, and the likes are your subheading tags. They guide your readers and help them know where and what to read. You can make use of LSI keywords in your subheadings; they are very helpful.

- Title Tag: Including your primary keyword in your title tag is very important. You can also add your LSI keywords in your title tag.

- First and last paragraph: LSI keywords can attract your visitors since they are associated with the topic; they are interested in. LSI keywords can be used at the beginning and the end of your article.

Get Links from Authority Sites and Reliable Sources

If you are worried about how you can generate huge traffic for your website and you are tired of this problem, then it could be a backlink problem. You can build your backlinks when you have achieved the following:

- You create high-quality and engaging content.

- You include LSI keywords in your content.

What does Link Juice mean?

Link juice describes the ranking power a website can pass to another site. It begins with Domain Authority (DA). According to Google, every website has a general Domain Authority, your domain will have more power when your DA is higher, and your posts will rank easily.

Every page also has a Page Authority number. The Page Authority evaluates the strength of each page. Most times, higher PA helps you rank more in the search engines. Several factors affect the page authority. The number of backlinks at the domain, the Domain Authority of the genuine domain, and social engagement determine the page authority.

For instance, if there is Site D and Site F. The ranking factor works the same way across both websites. If site D has a link pointing to it, while site F has no links, then site D will rank more in the search engines as a result of an external link flowing towards the site.

If link juice flows in both sides, sites that link to site D will as well link to other websites.

Link Building Strategies

- There are some things you need to know about link building. Below are some tips about link building.

- Backlinks should have relevant anchor text.

- Almost 25 percent of your anchor text should be your website's name.

- Backlinks building should follow a slow and steady process.

- With good on-page optimization, you will get good quality from your backlinks.

Creating an Email List for Traffic

If you want to own a successful website, one of the things that will help you to achieve that is creating an Email list. Creating an email list helps to generate more traffic to your website and also build a good relationship with your readers. This will help to boost your website business. Your email list will be a long-term asset for your business.

Below are ways to make your website generate email list:

- Utilize lead boxes: Most readers dislike pop-ups. They could be very annoying, distracting, and can be very difficult to close. Pop-ups can be incorporated by utilizing LeadBoxes. You can increase your email list by utilizing LeadBoxes wisely.

- Opt-in forms: If you want to create an email list without stress, you can include an opt-in form to your website. If you have a WordPress site, you will find it easy to do this. Thrive Leads is one of the most effective tools that offer you different opt-in forms you can include on your website.

- Developing landing pages: You can develop a landing page with the use of a landing page builder such as Thrive Architect or develop a landing page with the use of a WordPress theme.

Update Your Old Content

Another important factor that can help you generate traffic on your website is updating your old content. Your old content can still drive traffic to your website if you keep updating them. Some information is dynamic; therefore, you need to keep updating your post to have the latest development.

You can bring life and vibe to your old content by:

- Recycling old posts.

- Updating and improving old content

- Creating evergreen content like tips, how-to, and more.

How to Update Old Content

You should update your old content if you want to generate more traffic. Below are ways you can update your old content.

- Update images and media: If the pictures you used for your old contents are out of date, your readers will think that the remaining content is also outdated. Ensure you update all old images and use images that are recent.

- Add new statistics: Data changes a lot. If your content is still quoting a source from 2013, then it is high time you updated your sources. Ensure the information you update is from recent sources.

- Improve the content's structure: Your content's structure will get your readers stuck to the screen. Make sure your older content continues to be engaging, well-detailed, and interesting. You can also improve your content's structure by including new bullets, subheadings, and links.

- Include internal links to old posts: You can include some links to older content on your website.

Guest Blogging

Guest blogging is used by website owners to boost traffic to their websites. Guest blogging is one of the most powerful tool's website owners use to improve their domain authority. Guest blogging is the act of writing for another website in their industry. Guest bloggers get links for their website in exchange for a piece of content written.

Guest blogging provides a lot of benefits to website owners. When you display your professionalism on other websites, you can make your site as an authority figure and create healthy relationships with other professionals in your field.

There are some criteria that determine your content's quality. When guest blogging, ensure your expertise show in your content, write posts that are free of grammatical mistakes, add links that give reliable information on your post's topic.

Inviting guest posts on your website will help you offer new and fresh content to your readers. If you want to keep your audience engaged and boost your website, then guest blogging is for you. When searching for sites that accept guest posts, you should consider the following:

- Ensure the site is within your niche.

- The site is active online.

- The site has good Domain Authority.

How your website can rank number 1 on the Internet

It is a different case when you have visitors on your website and a different one when your website ranks number one. Every website and business owner aims to rank number one on the Internet. This is because ranking number one would help you generate more traffic to your website, increase your visibility, and get more profits. This section discusses what SEO is and what to do to rank number one on the Internet.

Search Engine Optimization

When we talk about SEO (search engine optimization), it expands the visibility of a website in the search results. SEO has helped lots of websites to rank more pages in Search Engine Result Pages SERPs and, as such, generate more traffic to the website.

SEO is often regarded as a strategy taken by website owners to ensure that their blogs pop out in the search engine. SEO does two things, which are visibility and rankings. Visibility shows the extent to which a particular domain is prominent in search engine results. Your domain will become prominent in search engine results when there is high visibility.

Rankings describe how search engines determine where a particular web page can be placed in SERPs. There are certain things you need to do improve your ranking on the Internet. The thing is that high rankings do not just occur like that, even some well-skilled and experienced website owners still struggle to reach the top spot.

SEO helps to make your pages visible and relevant. Ranking number 1 on Google is associated with so many factors. One of the ways you can rank number 1 is by building a good reputation online. Below are ways to improve your rankings.

Factors that Help You Rank Number 1

Page Speed

Page speed is one of the major factors for SEO ranking. Google seeks to improve the experience of users on the web. According to Google, if your website refuses to load fast, it could be penalized.

Rankbrain

According to Google, RankBrain is one of the most important factors that contribute to top rankings. RankBrain uses Artificial Intelligence in its search results. After content and links, the next important ranking factor is RankBrain.

This search engine helps Google to set search results and offer users more search results. There are other signals like bounce rate, dwell time and a clickthrough rate that affect search engine ranking.

Dwell time refers to how long your visitors stay on your website. The bounce rate refers to the number of people that left your website because they couldn't get what they wanted. Clickthrough rate refers to the percentage of the audience that clicks to visit your website.

Content and Keywords

The content of your article and your keywords contribute to ranking. Your H1 tag, Description tag, URL, Title tag, and image alt text are what you should pay attention to if you want your website to rank as number 1 on Google.

You can utilize keywords in some places on your page. You should utilize your keywords in several places within your content. Google ranks websites with comprehensive and creative content faster. Therefore, pay attention to your content and keywords.

Social Signals

Another factor that helps your website to rank number 1 is social signals. When your content is being shared on social networks, it shows that your content is valuable. According to an SEO study, there is an association between social shares and search engine ranking. When your content is shared, it helps to improve your search engine rankings.

Metadata

During website development, every page is created in a way that there is a space to insert details about your content or metadata. You should update and review Metadata over time. There are different types of metadata; title metadata, description metadata, and keyword metadata.

The title metadata is the most important metadata on your web page; it helps to display page titles at the top of a browser. The description metadata is the window display of your website. A nice Meta description will have two full sentences.

CHAPTER TWELVE

Search Engine Optimization (SEO) Glossary

Acquisition

Acquisition in online marketing can be referred to as an action which a business intends to achieve. For instance, if a business offers different plans for subscription, [the registration process would be seen as the company's acquisition, as this is what the company hopes to achieve via its strategy.

Algorithm

An algorithm can be referred to as a computer program that is used by search engines to search for signals and clues, which helps them deliver to the users, relevant and useful search results.

Alt text

This is the short form for Alternative text, and this can be referred to as a phrase or word that is fitted in as an attribute element that comes in HTML, which describes an image. Since images cannot be crawled by the search engines, they make use of alt text to index any content and then reveal it anytime any relevant search is performed. Online users also have access to this alt text, if due to some reasons, the image fails to show or load on the web page.

Anchor text

This text is a clickable and visible text that is usually hyperlinked. The words inscribed inside this text is said to be one of the major factors determining the ranking of a website in the result pages of search engines.

Analytics

Analytics has to do with the data collection linked to the performance of a website in terms of page views, visit duration, visits, bounce rates, etc. Analytics can be used in comprehending the visitors' behavior and your website's performance, which permits improvements in these aspects.

Backlink

A backlink refers to links from another site. Backlinks are also referred to as incoming links or inbound links.

Branding

Branding can be referred to as creating a unique image and name for a product so as to establish a position among the customers and on the market. This process is mainly achieved via different advertising campaigns, both offline and online.

Bing Ads

This is an online program that enables users to create campaigns for advertisement on the Bing search engine.

Broken link

Broken links don't work, which means that the link will lead to a page that doesn't exist, most probably because the page has been deleted or moved.

Browser

Web browser or simply browser is an application that is used in finding and displaying content on the web.

Cache

This is the component that stores the data from sites which the user has visited.

Competitiveness

This is also referred to as keyword competition, which measures how difficult a website can be positioned for a particular keyword, with reference to its competitors, i.e., websites using the same keyword to rank their websites as well. Keyword competitiveness has to do with how popular the keyword is, as well as how competitive the sector is.

Content

When we talk of SEO, the content has to do with any information published on a site, which is created to attract search engine traffic. Different content types can be utilized like videos, product pages, images, blog posts, guides, lists, articles, etc. Content plays a vital role in positioning a website today.

Canonical tag

This is used in handling duplicate content. It tells the search engines which page should be handled as a copy of a different URL. Also, search engines should credit the initial page when adding these pages to search results.

Conversion

This has to do with that particular action you want your browsers/web visitors to take like sign up, sale, file downloading, etc.

Crawler

This is a program utilized by the search engines to visit websites and retrieve information for the index of search engines.

Cryptic text

This is the text making use of a certain code.

CTR

The full meaning of CTR is click-through rate, which is used in measuring how successful an online campaign is like an email marketing campaign or advertising campaign. The click-through rate can be calculated by dividing the number of clicks by the number of impressions.

CSS

CSS refers to Cascading Style Sheets, who resent the language that is used in describing formatting and look of a document that is written in a markup language. The page is affected by the CSS in terms of fonts, color, and layout.

Domain Authority

This is used in describing how domain name strength is measured. The domain authority value is influenced by three major factors, such as size, popularity, and age. This ranges between the values of 0 and 100.

Flash

This can be referred to as a technology used in creating interactive multimedia applications like games, banners, websites, etc. When we talk of websites, they usually make use of Flash technology in displaying an animated video or a photo gallery. While visual effects do well in improving a website's visual aspect, one pitfall of this technology is that search engines cannot index the flash's contents. Aside from this, the technology can lengthen the time a website loads.

Follower

This is someone that subscribes so as to get some notifications on your updates. When we talk of social media, these followers are users of social media that decided to follow your account, by clicking the subscribe, follow, or like button.

GIF

This is the short form for Graphic Interchange Format. This image file has a lower quality compared to other format types; however, it supports animations. These file sizes are small, which makes them great for websites. However, the color palette seems to be more limited compared to that of other types of images.

Google AdWords

This is an advertising program that is provided by Google. It functions mainly to help you set up and perform online advertising with result pages of search engines showing sponsored results.

Homepage

This is called the website's introductory page. This is the first page visited by a user when the domain of a website is typed into the browser. The homepage can also be referred to as the main page or index page.

HTML

This means Hypertext Markup Language, which represents the standard system for the tagging of text files, so as to change the page's structure like photos, tables, headings, text, etc.).

Hyperlink

This refers to a link reference that permits the user of the website to access a different document or an important section of the document.

Inbound link

This is also called a backlink. An inbound link is a link on a different website that points to a particular page on your site.

Index

The search engine index has to do with the gathering of information obtained by the search engine crawlers. This data collection gathered in the index is now used to give answers to search queries.

Indexable

This refers to web pages, websites, or the content of a site that search engines can index because it follows the guidelines set by the search engines. By this, the algorithms of these search engines can crawl and index a website's contents successfully, so as to maximize the advantages of an online presence.

Interact

Interacting in online marketing terms refers to some form of conversation with your social followers, visitors to your website, etc.

Internet marketing

This is also referred to as online marketing. This has to do marketing that makes use of online media like social media, online advertising, and a website, etc. with plans to generate leads and promote a business.

Java

This is a programming language that is used in creating applications that can function on virtual browsers and machines.

Java applets

These are java applications that can be easily downloaded from the server and then run on a Java-compatible web browser.

JavaScript

This is the scripting language used in a website's HTML file

****

This is also called JPEG, which is the full meaning of the Joint Photographic Experts Group. This file is used mainly for graphics. It lets users create high-quality images that can then be resized; however, the image's quality will be damaged after it is resized.

Keyword

A keyword can be referred to as a phrase or word used in describing a web page's content. Keywords are included in SEO to ensure the web page is optimized, but they are used in paid advertisements as well.

Keyword density

This refers to the number of times a keyword or keyword phrase is used on the webpage.

Landing page

This is a single page that comes up anytime a user clicks the link in the results from search engines, links that are posted on different social media platforms, search engine ads, added to the email campaign, etc. You can also call this page the lander or the lead capture page.

Link

A link connects two points. Most times, it is inserted into a picture or a highlighted word that can be clicked so that the user can be taken to another object. Links come in different types.

Metatag

This is utilized in HTML to mark up the site's content so that search engines can understand the data. Metatags provide information about the HTML document.

Metrics

These are measures that help to keep track of a specific element. Metrics like average session time, number of visits, etc. can be tracked. Metrics help to evaluate and analyze the performance of the website.

Mobile-friendly

A website is said to be mobile-friendly if the content is easily and correctly displayed on mobile devices like tablets, smartphones, multimedia phones, etc.

Metadata

This provides details about the web page utilizing the standardized tags and language that enable search engines to interpret the data.

Negative keyword

This type of keywords is utilized for controlling the online advertising campaign. Negative keywords are used to avoid any ads related to irrelevant searches popping out; this helps to improve the advertising campaign's performance.

Online presence

Online presence describes when a business is promoted with the use of online media like social media accounts, search engine ads, websites, etc. Online presence helps to get in touch with the online audience by creating an online strategy to improve your website.

Optimization

Optimization refers to the act of abiding by SEO guidelines in order to improve a website's performance and ranking in the search engine results. You can optimize different parts of a website, aspects like title optimization, video optimization, content optimization, image optimization, etc. can be done.

Off-page

This describes the factors that determine a website's ranking. These factors are not on the website; they are external factors.

On-page

This describes factors that determine the ranking of a website. These factors are internal factors available on the website. They include content, tags, keywords, etc.

Organic reach

This refers to the number of people who viewed your post via unpaid distribution.

Page rank

This ranges between 0 and 1; it enables Google to identify a website's importance. Google search algorithm utilizes this metric to know how relevant the results associated with the search query are.

PPC

This means pay-per-click; it describes a kind of paid advertising utilized in online marketing.

Ranking

This shows the position a website appears due to a search query. If the website ranked among the top searches, the website would generate more visits. The ranking is a vital aspect of search engine optimization.

Referral

This explains how a page relates to another page.

Search engine protocol

This is an application that enables search engines to get information from the Internet so as to present search engine results. The language and the techniques used by search engine protocol are understood and recognized by the search engines.

Traffic

This means how data flow on the website. Traffic in the website world describes how much data is received and sent by users that visit that website.

User experience

User experience describes the experience acquired by a person while utilizing an application or a website. User experiences influence the way a product is viewed. It also describes the satisfaction derived by a person for using a product.

Conclusion

Getting 500 visitors daily and ranking number one on the Internet is no easy task. This is why we've taken our time to write this book to help you achieve this feat. Different SEO techniques, as well as the do's and don'ts, are also included. However, we are sure that by adhering to the rules and ideas written in this guide, you'll see great results.

www.ingramcontent.com/pod-product-compliance
Lightning Source LLC
La Vergne TN
LVHW051248050326
832903LV00028B/2641